Necessary Changes

A Guide through the Four Seasons of Life

Dr. Preston Williams II

iUniverse, Inc.

New York   Bloomington

Necessary Changes
A Guide through the Four Seasons of Life

iUniverse books may be ordered through booksellers or by contacting:

iUniverse
1663 Liberty Drive
Bloomington, IN 47403
www.iuniverse.com
1-800-Authors (1-800-288-4677)

ISBN: 978-1-4401-4456-1 (sc)
ISBN: 978-1-4401-4458-5 (hc)
ISBN: 978-1-4401-4457-8 (ebook)

Printed in the United States of America

iUniverse rev. date: 06/22/2009

Dedication

From my desire to know someone special while seeking the greater challenge to know myself, I dedicate this book to someone who has never sought public recognition and would never approve of such acknowledgment. Our paths first crossed in 1976, thirty-three years ago, during our early teenage years. After graduating from high school, I lost touch with you—until most recently. After over three decades of being separated by time, demographics, and our unique personal experiences in life, destiny has once more allowed our paths to cross, this time in a most significant way. I honor you with partial anonymity.

To my fiancée, Kathy Elaine, an amazing woman whom I love dearly and owe the delight of knowing as a very special friend, confidante, and source of inspiration, who in her love and kindness forces me to continue to struggle with truths that are not so self-evident. Thank you for sharing your incredible life story with me and for opening your heart once more to share a life with me. Your courage to endure and conquer life's most challenging moments has inspired me immensely—you have forever changed my life.

Contents

Acknowledgments

Like most books, this one didn't just happen. From several years of lectures, seminars, and sermons, it grew slowly. From tender roots planted in well-prepared soil, *Necessary Changes* sprouted, leafed, budded, and blossomed. It has been a very special project, brought to fruition through observations, research, and personal experiences. It is a reflection of what has happened to all of us at some point in our lives. I want to express my deepest thanks to Ariel Hudson, who gave valuable, patient editorial and content suggestions along the way. Your commitment and sense of mission move me and have been a tremendous blessing.

In addition to speaking engagements, facilitating leadership seminars, theological lectures, and counseling, I am administrator of a Christian academy. Therefore, writing is never the first priority in my life. My writing takes place in the in-between hours of the day and night. This is made possible because of the people of excellence around me. As my administrative assistant at Gateway Christian Academy, Maxine Knight, manages much of my office procedures. She interacts daily with many requests that come to my desk. Her commitment to details and her gracious personality make it possible for me to retreat from my busy schedule and write. Thank you.

I wish to thank two very important people who I have had the distinct privilege of knowing over the past four years. The late Dr. N. G. Hyatt, Senior Pastor and founder of Gateway Church and Gateway Christian Academy, and his lovely wife, Lady N. R. Hyatt, Executive Director of Gateway Christian Academy. Dr. N. G. Hyatt, with a winsome spirit of excellence, has left an indelible imprint on my life. His ministry vision and dynamic leadership touched my life in a powerful and unique way. I am grateful for our brief moment in time and the opportunity to have known and served under this amazing leader.

Lady N. R. Hyatt, by her leadership and example, gives oversight and manages the affairs of the thriving ministry of Gateway Church with extraordinary expertise and is the Executive Director of Gateway Christian Academy, Ft. Lauderdale, Florida. I respect her highly for her tenacity, altruism, and strong leadership. Thank you for your consistent lifestyle of excellence and compassion.

I feel a deep sense of gratitude to my children and their families: Preston III and Portia Omega. Throughout the years, their love, encouragement, patience, and support during my many travels and involvements away from home have made it easy to fulfill my purpose in life.

To the reader, the fact that you've chosen this literature for your personal library says that you are a visionary who has the desire and the courage to change. Thanks for making this choice.

Finally, I specially thank God, my divine source and supplier of all that is possible, who gave me His Son, filled me with His love and inspired me to write this book—from His mind to my heart, which flows through my fingers to penning these pages.

Preface

This book is a revised and retitled edition of *The Seasons of Destiny's Perfection*, which was published in 2004. At the time of its publication, it was intended to be only an academic supplement to a series of life management seminars I was facilitating. Since that time, I was encouraged to fine-tune it and make it available to a broader audience. I did, and I am pleased to submit for your consideration, *Necessary Changes*. It is a summation of maturing ideas garnered from twenty-eight years of service in the "people business." It is a collaboration of the trials and joys I experienced. It is a work birthed not only from the solitary moments of a writer's retreat, but rather, in the midst of living. It is a collection of thoughts that I've pondered, researched, and studied. The principles I will share with you are influenced by great thinkers and mentors I've admired. The ideas gradually emerged into illuminating principles that turned to convictions.

I have dedicated my adult life striving to help people become their very best "selves"—to gain the confidence and inner freedom derived from the struggles of life. We face lifelong challenges, and the struggle to conquer them is difficult. I can identify with your struggles in the arena of life, but I understand and accept that my struggles are necessary for my strides, and my setbacks are actually setups for the greater blessings that are apportioned to my life's journey. As a motivational speaker, my struggles earned me dividends as they helped me to better understand life and positioned me to motivate others.

I have read many books about life and its countless issues. I have lectured, ministered, and counseled on just about every aspect of life issues and interpersonal relationships. So as I began this manuscript, I wanted to compose a book that would be different from others on the topic of life and the changes that are necessary to having a winning attitude toward life. It needed to be a book that placed life experiences into simple, practical context. In my opinion, once something is understood, a "current of peace" is released. This current of peace opens up our minds and hearts for meaningful actions, which will ultimately lead to progress at its best and good success.

Simply put, *Necessary Changes* is about life management. It is a manual of understanding why you are going through what you're going through at this time in your life. It is about your relationship with yourself, your friends, your loved ones, and the choices you must make at different points during your journey toward becoming the best you there can be. It is about changing those things in your life that can be changed and accepting those you cannot change, and trusting God with everything.

Throughout this book, you will be thoroughly introduced to the major theme of *Necessary Changes*, called the seasons of life. I strongly urge you to read with analytical thinking as I parallel the four seasons of nature with the four seasons we go must go through in life. Although I share a few life experiences, I did not fill this manuscript with stories. I wanted to get right to point. When you're at the end of your proverbial "rope," you need straight talk—forward-thinking principles that are critical for successful life transition. My goal is that while you are reading, you will begin to see your life situations from a purposeful perspective. Additionally, you will be challenged to open your mind and heart to the prospect of making the necessary changes that will make your life more fulfilling and pleasurable for yourself as well as those who will intersect your life daily.

Introduction

There is a time for everything, and a season for every activity under heaven.
I have seen the burden God has laid on men.
He has made everything beautiful
In its time.

—Ecclesiastes 3:1, 10, 11; NIV

Change — to undergo transformation, transition, or substitution <winter *changed* to spring>; suggests a difference that limits, restricts, or adapts to a new purpose; stresses a breaking away from sameness, duplication, or exact repetition <*vary* your daily routine>; to awaken <spiritual insight concerning a circumstance, issues, or person provoking re-evaluation >.

He who looks outside dreams, he who looks inside awakens.

—Carl Jung

Understanding Life Through Changing Seasons

I grew up in St. Marys, a small town in southeast Georgia. During my childhood, the simple and unique lifestyle of St. Marys challenged me to observe and embrace the magnificence and splendor of natural events, things that some would probably overlook or take for granted. Events like the miracle of the consistent seasonal changes and how they appeal to all the senses, its annual cycles, the diverse scents and colors that accompanied each season, the order of nature and its ability to maintain perfect harmony, and the comfort I felt as I stared out my window into the stillness of the night's soothing embrace. This brought a tremendous amount of stability to my young life.

During those early years of my childhood, I became conscious that somehow nature and mankind were significantly paralleled and related to one another. Now an adult, I realize the magnitude of this truth. *We all, in our own way, are searching for meaning.* This search takes us through the wilderness of various philosophies and religious experiences. Finally, we're at a place within ourselves that we hold suspect—the person we've become. Deep in our innermost being, we know that somewhere, somehow, we've missed an important truth that could have impacted our lives differently and brought clarity to the issues of life we now question. Because of this missing piece of unknown truth, we struggle to understand the matrix of our past. We're emotionally paralyzed by the numbness of our present facade, and our future is one haunting question that confronts us daily in the areas that represent the heartbeat of our existence: life, love, and relationships. Hence, we're left to deal with the ever-popular question, Why am I going through this?

As I travel, I'm presented with the opportunity of meeting and interacting with individuals from diverse backgrounds and different schools of thought. Based on discussion, in relation to the way individuals view life as a whole, I realize that my personal consensus of humanities' concerns about life and the reason for their existence is as accurate today as it was when I, too, questioned my experiences and the significance of my "being." During speaking and lecturing in different settings, it occurred to me that there was a resounding hunger to understand the meaning of certain experiences that seem to come and go and sometimes keep recurring without resolve or understanding. During casual conversation, individuals would share with me that life was similar to a treadmill, likening it to a vicious cycle to which they were sentenced. Some remarked that they were making lots of movement but weren't going anywhere. We all, at one point or another, can identify with similar questionable feelings.

In life, we go through seasons that seem so wasteful and unnecessary. When it is all said and done, we're left with this tiresome feeling that questions the "why" of life. Not understanding *why* we go through *what* we go through is a heart-wrenching experience. Sometimes, the frustration of life is so burdensome that we're tempted to curse the day we were born. Job, an Old Testament patriarch, understood such feelings. Amid his personal turmoil, he said to God, "Let the day perish wherein I was born, and the night in which it was said, there is a man child conceived" (Job 3:3). The search for understanding life's ups and downs is endless and, in many cases, even futile. Like the dry, dusty throat of a thirsty man lost in a desert, we reach for so many solutions and philosophies that we suppose will quench this thirst. To our dismay, we find ourselves drinking the dust of disillusionment. Empty and discouraged, we throw up our hands in defeat and resort to merely existing in this life. Herein lies the inevitable birthing of the attitude *que sera, sera*, whatever will be, will be. In theological circles, this attitude/philosophy is described as fatalism.

Fatalism does not encourage understanding nor does it enforce the pursuit of purpose. Fatalism implies that we are all subject to life without the benefit of personal choice—life without our cooperation and the intentional pursuit of purpose. Purpose is best known as one's destiny. To understand destiny is to embrace the fact that your life has been predetermined or predestined. When you embrace this fact, you must also embrace the fact that nothing occurs in life without reason or purpose. Without proper direction, we live our lives never knowing the purpose or reason for our experiences, whether good or bad. Knowing and understanding the reason for these experiences will ease the pressures of life and place all events, good or bad, in their proper perspective. Proper perspective may be defined as *the view in which an idea or experience fits that brings completeness, ease, and understanding.*

Perspective, therefore, must be ascribed to a legitimate nurturing source of understanding before it can be considered *proper.* Not every perspective is proper, especially in our search for the why of life. The most common mistake made by the seekers of truth and meaning is to look for the answers to the questions in life from life itself. The key to understanding life is not in life itself, but in the source of life. So our search should begin with understanding the source of life, for in this search, we will understand the origin and purpose of life. Everything that exists has a beginning, and since it has a beginning, then it is safe to assume that there was an intended purpose. Purpose began as an idea in the mind of God, the source. A plan for the idea was laid and then initiated. But before the idea, plan, and the purpose, there existed something much more important, the void. The void can be described as the emptiness or the need and necessity is the mother of invention (creation). Everything that is, is because of something or someone that exists but is incomplete (necessity).

If we apply these statements to life, it will be clear that life can be understood only through the source of life and that if life was given, there was first a need or a void to be filled. After this, *the idea* (you) came into the scheme of eternal planning as the means to which the need will be filled. This need, in turn, created the purpose for your existence. The plan represents the course upon which all events will take place. In essence, it is the road that you must travel that will prepare, shape, and define you for your purpose.

Let me briefly pause to express my belief as it relates to the pursuit of purpose, which is a vital element. I embrace the concept that this road to fulfilling our purpose is a continuum. There are many other purposes that we are fulfilling along the way. Clearly stated, I believe that while we are being prepared, shaped, and defined on this predetermined road through life's experiences such as love and relationships, we are also fulfilling intermediate purposes that lead us to our ultimate purpose in life. Simply put, our ultimate purpose is the sum total of all that we are to accomplish in life, but intermediate purposes are achieved at different times in life based on our level of maturity.

This level of maturity is determined by how well we learn from the events we encounter in life. Events are experiences we live out in life. They are divinely prearranged to fit within seasons. It is when one understands the concept of events within the realm of seasons one begins the journey of understanding the why of life. This understanding will bring ease to the frustration, uncertainty, and mystery of life. Then comes the acceptance that everything we encounter in life is simply a part of the perfecting process of life itself. This process is preparation for maximum living and our effective functioning in this world.

I do not intend to emphasize prosperity in this manuscript as it relates to the already overemphasized message of wealth and financial gain in the arena of personal empowerment and spiritual development. However, it is important that I establish at the initial stage that I believe in the principle of prosperity. To me, prosperity is the residual effect of the perfecting process experienced in the seasonal changes in life. I further contend that prosperity is much more than the acquisition of assets, liquid or tangible. It is a much deeper valuation of self. For this reason, assets should not be the consuming focus in your life, nor should it be an issue of constant concern; it should just *be* as a result of your earnest pursuit of knowing and fulfilling your purpose.

In Matthew 6:33, Christ declares, "But seek ye first the kingdom of God and His righteousness, and all of these things will be added unto you." Therefore, our objective in life should be to pursue that which is considered the proper perspective (that which is right in the eyes of God, our source). This will allow the prosperity that has already been predetermined and assigned to our journey in life, to be released in our lives at the time and place intended. So my emphasis will not be toward the effect, which is prosperity, but rather on the cause, which is destiny, as well as the seasons involved in the process of destiny's perfection.

King Solomon wrote, "To everything there is a season, and a time to every purpose under the heaven" (Ecclesiastes 3:1). By divine authorization, this wise king was sharing with the world a principle for understanding the mystery of life's eventful journey. This principle affirms that the divine plan of life consists of these two facts: (1) everything we experience in life has been assigned to specific seasons, (2) like the natural seasons of the earth, they are timed to fulfill a specific purpose on the road of destiny. In reality, nothing is by chance. Everything has a purpose. Whatever you're experiencing in life, whether negative or positive, it is for your good. Therefore, know that the season you're experiencing this very moment will not last forever; it is on a divine timer that is due to expire at the point of achieving its assigned purpose.

God, the source of life, is the mastermind behind all that exist, and so we shall parallel the revolving seasons of nature (summer, fall, winter, and spring) with the seasons involved in the process of personal growth and spiritual maturity. The objective is to bring clarity to *why* you are *where* you are at this point in your life, and to raise your level of enthusiasm toward pursuing life with a deeper sense of meaning.

Pivotal Road
Preston Williams II

I see a different road leading me …
Leading me somewhere distant, far beyond
My zones of comfort.

On this road I'm dancing …
Dancing the dance of cautioned freedom;
Romancing the experience, the risk of life,
Embracing the travel time moment-by-moment.

No familiar landmarks of my parents' time.
Their directions, points of interest all seem
Misplaced on this road I travel.

I see a sign ahead on this road I travel:
"NO U-TURNS ALLOWED
VIOLATORS WILL BE PROSECUTED,
UP TO A LIFETIME OF MENTAL IMPRISONMENT."

How long shall I travel this road I see?
To its end or mine?
Somehow this road and I
Are harmoniously
One.

Part I
Summer: The Season of Hardships

But if I go to the east, he is not there; if I go to the west,
I do not find him.
When he is at work in the north,
I do not see him; when he turns to the south,
I catch no glimpse of him.
But he knows the way that I take; when he has tested
Me, I will come forth as gold.

—Job 23:8–10 NIV

1

The Heat of Summer:
The Trials of Life and Their
Purpose

Summer's beauty is the extended beauty of spring, yet behind the beauty of spring and the clear sun-filled skies lay infestations, insects and rodents that were forced underground due to the coldness of winter. It is during the summer season that the temperature reaches a high that summons these elements to the earth's surface. The heat penetrates the cocoons where they slumbered to escape the winter chills, and now they resurface. The bacteria rise and infect the vegetation; the rodents and insects nibble away at nature's structures. Our homes and yards begin to show evidence of the hidden parasites. What was once invisible is now visible. The heat is sometimes so unbearable, and the ultraviolet rays so high, that prolonged exposure can cause skin cancer. We stand in amazement as we observe the pros and cons of the changing seasons. Yet, it is clear that certain precautions must now be initiated for preservation and continued growth.

I find the parallel between the trials of life and the season of summer profoundly similar. I doubt anyone will disagree with me when I say that life can present some tough experiences. The hardships and trials of life can make individuals feel as if they are in the unquenchable flames of an unending furnace. Confronted with these tough experiences, anyone would feel as if he has been forced to the end of his proverbial rope. And why not? You have awakened to the fact that you are in "the kitchen of life" ... and it is *hot*! Nothing seems to make sense any more. The plans you've made are foiled by unforeseen setbacks. Attempts to correct and bring resolution to your dilemma are crushed. A spouse threatens to leave the family that was built on love and trust. The children are in disarray and are courting the spirit of rebellion. Your career is uncertain due to downsizing, and financial stability is challenged. And you think, "If it isn't one thing, it's another." You've exhausted your means, and now you're mentally, emotionally, and physically depleted. You are left with nothing but a broken spirit and a sorrowful heart. Does this sound familiar?

Many individuals faced with these circumstances become frustrated with life. They resort to making decisions that could worsen their situation. Experience teaches me that the major problem these individuals encounter is the lack of proper guidance and the knowledge necessary for making informed decisions. The Bible tells us that people perish due to lack of knowledge (Hosea 4:6). Greek philosophers, scholars, and prophets of old have admonished humanity to ensure that in addition to all that we acquire in life, get "understanding" (Proverbs 4:7).

The summer season of life sensitizes us to crucial missing principle of understanding. Our inability to understand what lurks beneath the crust of our lives may cause us to live life in a blur of frustration. Understanding will cause a door to open within us, giving rise to a new dimension, a new life. This dimension serves as an X-ray of our symptomatic present condition that alerts us that something is wrong or displaced.

Many hardships are due to issues we are aware of but have chosen to ignore. Why? We simply don't want to deal with them. The unresolved issues we thought would just work out eventually never did. The abusive relationships keep resurfacing, yet you fail to address them. I think you get the idea. These are just a few of the issues that your summer season has now forced you to confront. These must be dealt with before destiny allows you to advance to the next level.

When you have been through the fire,
You will come out as pure gold.

—Job 23:10

The refining fire of our summer season in life creeps upon us as an intruder, seeking to steal away our peace, prosperity, and well being. Within the experience of hardships and trials exists a deeper meaning and purpose. I personally, have questioned this concept in the earlier years of my life. At first, it was truly difficult. How could I possibly fathom meaning in suffering, pain, loss, and despair? Human nature will not readily allow our minds to embrace this truth which serves as a maintenance mechanism of life. As was mentioned earlier, each season has a divine purpose and is timed with a date of completion. Unfortunately, we do not determine the date of completion per se. The commencement of seasons is determined by our destiny and purpose in life.

Metaphorically speaking, the heat of our life's summer season unfolds the deep, secret issues of our heart and that affects our lives, hence, our forward movement. In order to understand this concept, we must be aware that heat is more than an ideal temperature for various activities and recreations. At this point, heat takes on the form of a purifying agent of destiny. It penetrates the hardness of our hearts and creates openness to the counsel of the truth. Humanity has been admonished to "fall on the stone (Truth) and be broken" (Matthew 21:44). Truth is the corrective voice of the One who transcends His own creation, the One who professes to be ultimate reality, the personal God who gives us life and meaning and who calls us to be His expression of greatness in the world.

Truth is the foundation of destiny and the fuel of purpose. It is truth that seeks a place in our lives, like a parent whose tender, loving, caring heart is knitted to the child. Truth allows a season of correction. Truth knows our intention and purpose for existence and desires to mold us into our best selves. This is achieved through the refining fire of the summer season of life. The refining fire is not for our annihilation but for the breaking, melting, and molding of our hardened selves. The expressed purpose of this process is for rebuilding or reshaping our lives for maximum living.

The revealing voice of summer's experiences focuses our attention on innate infestations of the soul. From the very beginning, I expressed my intention of paralleling the seasons of nature with the seasons of life. These progressive parallels will assist us in our understanding of the changes that we all must go through in life. To continue that process, I'd like to deal with the issue of infestation. In nature, infestation is seen as a by-product of the presence of parasites. These parasites have been forced to the surface from the crevices of the earth by the sweltering heat of summer. There are many parasites that are exposed during the summer. I will focus on one type in particular and refer to these specific parasites as aphids as I further discuss and equate the trials of life with the season of summer.

Many hardships are due to issues we are aware of but have chosen to ignore

Here I offer a brief description/synopsis of them. They are very unique parasites and will be ideal in properly developing my parallel. The aphid is a common name for any of a large group of insects, which are more popularly known as plant lice or green flies. Aphids are commonly found on the roots, leaves, and stems of plants. They frequently do great damage. The mouths of aphids are designed for piercing and sucking plants. Their presence is readily detected by marks, wrinkles, or abnormalities of the infested plant. Additionally, aphids emit from their anus a sweet glutinous substance called honeydew, which is eagerly sought by ants and other insects. It is important to note that ants may hide aphids and protect them from predators. As the paralleling of the seasons of nature with the seasons of life develops, the relevance of these parasites will come to light.

The description of aphids can be easily paralleled with the issues that have surfaced due to the trial season of summer in life. I quickly outline what the aphids represent in your situation. Consider this: *aphids* are the debilitating issues in life that eat away at our personhood, abilities, body, soul, and spirit. These debilitating issues affect the totality of our well-being. Although not an exhaustive list, the debilitating issues that confront humanity today can be identified as unhealthy relationships, obsessions, worshipped possessions, and negative thoughts. As was aforementioned, in nature, aphids are found on roots, leaves, and stems. These three locations are the attack centers for the aphids. They are very important to the continued life and productivity of plant system. The *roots* of a plant are the lifeline of existence. The *leaves* are the manifested life form of the plants, and the *stems* are the support systems of the plant life and are extensions of the root.

So let's parallel the picture of nature with that of life. The aphids in your life are the debilitating issues that have attached themselves to the lifeline or the nurturing center of your existence (roots). Because of this attachment, these debilitating issues now affect the manifestations of our lives: children, career, finance, and personal well-being (leaves).

Additionally, these issues flow over into our support systems: friends, family, and credible authorities in our lives (stems). The outcome can be, and sometime is, devastating! So then, the summer season is introduced in our lives to alert us of the undetected aphids that are lurking, ready to destroy us. So summer, the season of hardships and trials, is like a diagnostic system of sorts.

The three aspects of life mentioned above—root, leaves, and stems—are natural as well as normal in the scheme of nature. But when they are subjected to the presence of the aphids, these parasites distort their original intent, infecting them and causing abnormalities. Likewise, it is natural and normal for us to have certain experiences that contribute to our personal development as time passes. But life can take a wrong turn. We could find ourselves walking through life blinded by the illusions imposed on us by our support systems stems: family, friends, and those we deem credible authorities. These support systems may have our best interest at heart, but it is important to understand that not all advice will be sound or objective. Individuals with good intentions can be the facilitators of debilitating issues (aphids) that you've innocently allowed in your life. We shall explore this relational aspect later.

The refining fire is not for our annihilation, but for the breaking, melting, and molding of our hardened selves

The mouthparts of aphids are adapted for piercing and sucking plants. As was stated previously, the presence of aphids is readily detected by marks, wrinkles, or abnormalities on the infested plant. Likewise, our lives have been pierced and sucked from us as we adapt to the unhealthy conditions and the lethal everyday influences that we refer to as our comfort zones. Marked by limited success and marginal happiness, wrinkled with despair and hopelessness, and isolated mentally with abnormalities of insignificance and questioned abilities, life becomes an anxiety-ridden mystery. On the inside, you're feeling all of these mixed emotions, but you don't know why. Nothing is as frightening as the unknown, especially as it relates to your well-being. You have some ideas as to the reason for your dilemma, but then, uncertainty consumes your every thought. Fear grips the heart, resulting in hasty and unwise decisions, compounding life's many inevitable challenges.

The only remedy is *heat*. The heat of your experiences exposes the heartfelt issues for what they really are and the harm they're causing. There is a saying that I have heard from my childhood, "If you can't stand the heat, get out of the kitchen." I beg to differ in this regard. I believe this resolve to be the problem rather than the solution. The problem with this resolve is that we prematurely abort the divine process of heat (summer season/trials/hard times), hence abandoning the developmental stage critical to the progress of purposeful living. Rather than aborting the heated season, it would behoove us to embrace this season with a spirit of understanding. Doing so will allow destiny to fulfill its purpose in your life. Here are some questions to consider before you decide to prematurely abort the process:

- What do I need to come to terms with during this season in my life?
- Why am I dealing with this situation or circumstance at this point in my life?
- What areas of my life have been affected by these variables?
- What am I to do with this area of concern that has now been exposed?
- Am I open to change? If not, how do I prepare myself for what must be done?

These, and many other questions, will be dealt with throughout the following chapters, but for now, you must make the decision to endure the process and position your self for change.

The heat of the summer seasons of life will make most do what is seldom done, that is, *think*. I have found that many individuals don't want to think about life. Maybe they find life too disappointing to think about. To think or to ponder life is a way of evaluating where you are in life. This thinking or to pondering with a sober and balanced sense of personal management is like an antivirus system on a computer. It periodically scans the mind of the system (hard drive) for errors. If any are found during the scanning process, an alert message appears that identifies and corrects the error. This is the point where some individuals, unfortunately, opt to abort the process. The point of identifying and correcting the errors (debilitating issues) is where they prepare to exit the "kitchen." The heat is turned up and change is the ultimate resolve. Change is the prerequisite for attracting peace and well-being into every aspect of our lives.

Important Note: *Aborting the process does not terminate the season; it only suspends personal growth and the release of destiny's intended benefit in your life. The issues will continue to resurface at various points in your life until they are properly dealt with.*

At the eve of summer's heated confrontation, we enter into the next chapter of life. As we prepare to take on the challenge of life's next chapter, we must brace ourselves for the uneasiness of our conditioned nature to change. We should not be alarmed or discouraged if we feel somewhat apprehensive and uncertain. This is how the human nature responds. We feel this way only because we're treading on uncommon ground. We are about to leave that which has been defined in our hearts and minds as our *comfort zones.* Yes, it is a leap of faith into the unknown, but the payoff is phenomenal. The payoff cannot be measured in dollars and cents. The value is much more than that which is tangible.

Having crossed your own comfort zones to facilitate correction is personal growth at its best. Crossing comfort zones to facilitate change is an innate empowerment of self. It is the doorway to the corridors of truth that will bring a peace that will pass all understanding. Breaching comfort zones is prerequisite to discovering new experiences as well as personal growth. You discover you are, as I consider, "Dying to self." In essence, you're dying to a value system that has, heretofore, limited your ability to experience life at maximum levels. Consequently, you experience life in a constant state of feeling significant and fulfilled.

There is a final aspect of the summer parasites we've come to know as aphids. This aspect has to do with the relationship between aphids and ants. As was stated in my brief synopsis of aphids, I discovered that aphids emit from their anus a sweet glutinous substance called honeydew, which is eagerly sought by ants and other insects. Incidentally, because of this, ants may hide aphids and protect them from other predators.[1] Here lies the parallel to humanity. Aphids (debilitating issues) are protected by ants (individuals or mind-sets that embrace the sweet nectar of debilitating illusions of life). The ant (persons/mind-sets) will protect its interest (aphids: debilitating issues) from predators. Predators, in the eyes of the ant, can be paralleled with any thing or person that would render the aphid ineffective and unable to produce the sweet nectar of disillusionment that they feed upon. In this case, truth would be an enemy or predator to the aphid and the ant. Two parasites (debilitating mind-sets) join forces as a defense for preservation.

Within this sphere of thinking, it is apparent that once the heat of your summer season unearths the protectors of these debilitating issues, you will need to identify them quickly. Again, the purpose of the heat of summer is to bring to surface that which is common, hidden, and detrimental to maximizing life. Once these issues are exposed, what you do with the knowledge of their existence is the defining moment of your season of hardship and trial. In everyone's life, this season must come. And when it does, we're to see it through the eyes of God, our source. It is through His eyes that peace is possible no matter what season we find ourselves.

If we will, but for a moment, allow ourselves to transcend our learned behavior of distress during the summer/trial season of life and listen to the voice of truth, we will experience a burning, eternal promise of hope gripping our heart and soul. This eternal promise would come in the form of this decree: "All things (negative or positive) work together for your good, to those who are called according to His (God) purpose" (Romans 8:28).

The following poem was written by an unknown author. I think it sums up the attitude that we all should embrace as we encounter our summer season of hardships and trials. Whoever the author is, he or she has gained a healthy understanding of how to respond to the heat of trials and the sting of disappointment.

"Disappointment—His Appointment";
change one letter, then I see that the thwarting
of my purpose is God's better choice for me.
His appointment must be blessing
though it may come in disguise;
for the end, from the beginning,
open to His vision lies.

"Disappointment—His Appointment."
Whose? The Lord who loves me best, understands and
knows me fully, who my faith and love would test.
For like loving earthly parents He rejoices when
He knows that His child accepts unquestioned,
all that from His wisdom flows.

"Disappointment—His Appointment";
no good things will He withhold. From denials
oft we gather treasures of His love untold.
Well He knows each broken purpose leads to
a fuller, deeper trust, and the end of all
His dealings prove our God is wise and just.

"Disappointment—His Appointment";
Lord I take it then as such, like clay in the hands
of the potter yielding wholly to His touch.
My life's plan is all His molding; not one single
choice be mine. Let me answer unrepining,
"Father, not my will, but Thine."[2]

What a wonderful summation of how we should approach the trials of our lives. At the beginning of this chapter, I mentioned how unbearable the heat of summer can get. I am so enamored with the infinite and unconditional love of God, the source of life. Through God, truth speaks this word of promise, "I will not put (allow) more on you than you can bear." In essence, the intensity of life's circumstances and the dangerous levels of pressing situations will never be allowed to overcome us or to consume us. The process has been uniquely tempered and specifically tailored for our shaping.

Finally, let me emphasize that although we are to embrace the purpose of our season of hardships and trials, we will not find our joy in the heat of the flames or in the fuel being added to make the blaze hotter. If we did, as mentioned before, we would only want to be out of the situation; and we would abort the process. But by keeping our focus on the truth, the refiner of life who will never leave us unattended but is right there controlling the process and the heat of our trial, we will emerge at our summer's end with a sense of peace. We will come to terms with the critical issues of life we need to confront, and if we submit to the refining process for its completion, we will emerge knowing the *why* (purpose) concerning the season of summer in our lives.

2

Impurities Exposed: Identifying Your Debilitating Issues

Identifying the debilitating issues in our lives is an important aspect to finding healing to our season of trial. This chapter aims at exposing these issues and challenges you to come to terms with the fact that there are some people and perceptions you need to reevaluate. Our summertime heat revealed to us some very interesting but crucial information about ourselves. It made us pause to take a closer look at the people in our lives, the choices we've made, the perceptions and values we once embraced as truth, and our reason for living. Now that we've been empowered to examine these areas of our lives, we are faced with yet another challenge. The challenge seems simple when stated but complex and sometimes painful when initiated. Yet, it is a normal part of the process. So what is this challenge? It is being true to yourself about the knowledge you have gained regarding the people you held in high esteem and the startling reality that these individuals are part of the problem. It is being true to yourself that the perceptions you held as the "holy grail" of life are tainted by bravado and selfish social innuendoes.

During my early forties, I spent a great deal of time counseling individuals who suffered from the effects of substance abuse, a debilitating issue. Based on the information gleaned through the sessions, I discovered that although substance abuse was a critical issue, other underlying factors were the problem. Substance abuse was not the "root" debilitating issue; it was the "fruit." Likewise, many of my clients never had a substance abuse issue, but there were other root issues that spawned fruit in various areas. I refer to fruit like low self esteem, failure to maintain healthy relationships, emotional bankruptcy, and lack of personal identity. There was evidence of self-imposed social, economical, professional, and educational status.

These are lifelong issues that threaten to make living a chore. So, in the ensuing pages, we will explore how these roots, if allowed to go unchecked, nurture our tree of despair and bear the fruit that plague us throughout life. It is in the trial season of our lives that these root issues are exposed. We refrain from living in denial and face reality about what truth has exposed. The three undisputed and most influential areas that represent our most diligent of challenges in life are people, perceptions, and purpose unknown. Every problem in life can be attached to one of these three areas. Honestly speaking, no matter which one is the root issue, each one is affected eventually. The process of infestation is like creeping paralysis. If it goes unchecked and the initial symptoms are ignored, you become oblivious of the degree of damage. Unfortunately, when reality hits, it is too late for remediation.

The Influence of People

God is greater than man.
—Job 33:12*b*

The people we allow in our lives become our support, our voices of reason, and if I may say, our "second selves." All too often I have witnessed individuals who have lost themselves in other people's ideals. It is as though they live their lives through, and for, others. They place their lives, their future, and their happiness in the hands of mortals, who by definition are imperfect in and of themselves. Let me hasten to note that *there are individuals who can and will impart benefits into your life, whether in words or deeds.* So I am not implying that there should be no reliance on people. But there should be limitations.

Seeking deeper understanding of life through the ideals of individuals as your only source of hope is very limiting. Such a relationship creates a platform for dictatorial control. You distance yourself from the realm of ultimate truth. You become desensitized to the daily promptings of a higher authority. When one chooses the way of popular opinion instead of evoking spiritual guidance, distress is inevitable. These are individuals who have become stagnated because they did not seek spiritual guidance. Their lives lack luster due to the flawed finite thinking they spent time nurturing. Here is an undisputed truth: *No one has ever had his future or progress stifled from seeking the infinite wisdom of God.*

In comprehending the depth of the individuals to whom I refer, in regard to scrutinizing the voices of persons you allow in your life, I mean those who go beyond the line of personal advice. These individuals become dictators of your life and destiny. They consider themselves to be the prognosticators of relevant truth—imposing their values and convictions upon others but will not take responsibility for the results. These individuals refuse to acknowledge your uniqueness—God's imprint on your life. When we release our selves from the grip or control of others upon us, we open ourselves to the eternal attributes of God, the source. When we're released from stronghold of people, we experience a realm of abundant, harmonious, healthy, vital, and wholesome living. Unless we exercise our right to overcome these strongholds, we will find ourselves in constant struggle amid the summer season of trial and turmoil.

At this point, have you been able to identify such person or persons? Do you now agree that they placed a hold on your progress in life? Are they an immediate family member, a childhood or longtime friend, or a social/professional authority you deemed credible? Have you allowed anyone of questionable character to become connected to your heart, soul, and mind? Not withstanding, allowing someone to connect this way is not the real problem. The key element that creates the problem is when the connection is with the wrong person. In life we have a mixture of those who edify us and those who contaminate us. So, having this insight, what do you plan to do with what you have?

The trial season is a time for discernment. It is a time of sorting through the maze of influences to determine the degree to which we will allow different persons to participate in our arena of life. There is a wonderful portion of Scripture that I treasure and appropriate in my associations including personal relationships. It warns us to, "Mark/identify those who cause divisions … avoid them" (Romans 16:17). These are sound words, which confront the issue of corporate dysfunctional relationships caused by individuals with hidden agendas.

Let's apply this Scripture to a more personal context. The admonition is for us to watch out for individuals who cause personal disagreement, thus limiting our pursuit of purpose and our ability to become self-actualized. Mark those whose intent is to impose their personal agenda or values on you. For some it might be out of ignorance. Others might be fully aware of the debilitating results. This is the kind of individual who has caused you to sever harmony within yourself, and now you're experiencing the fruit of inner turmoil. You mark them to determine the degree to which you may associate with them in the future. You mark them to properly assess their credibility in your life. Determining the kind of role people are to play in your life is one of the most critical of all decisions you'll need to make in your seasons of personal growth (e.g., decision maker, facilitator, encourager, support system).

The Influence of Perceptions

We be not able to go up against the people; for they are stronger than we.

—Numbers 13:31*b*

And we were in our own sight as grasshoppers, and so we were in their sight.

—Numbers 13:33*b*

Perception—**a:** to attain awareness or understanding of **b:** to regard as being such <*perceived* threats> <was *perceived* as a loser>

How do you see yourself? How do others see you? Have you ever been told that you'll never amount to anything? Can you relate to the following statements: Negatively stated, "You're just like your father [or mother]," "You're a felon, you can only go but so far in this life," "Your teenage daughter is pregnant? Her life is over," "You're too old to be thinking about pursuing this or that," or "You're too young."

What about the things we say to ourselves? "I am an unlovable, worthless person," "Nobody will ever love me," "I'll never be able to change," "I've been a failure all my life," "I guess I'll always be a failure," "If people really knew me, they wouldn't like me." These are only a few of the debilitating perceptions that I've heard thrown around as if they were sanctioned prophetic utterances of destiny. Unfortunately, children, teenagers, and adults buy into these lethal nuggets, which begin the shaping of the person's perception of himself or herself. These perceptions, if not properly addressed, will advance into adulthood and mature into more debilitating issues.

The fuel of decision making can be summed up in one word: perception. The most debilitating issue revealed during your summer/trial season is a tainted misguided perception. Perception bridges the gap between people and purpose. People shape perception, and perception determines whether or not you move forward to, or retreat from your purpose in life. An in-depth understanding of what forms perception will help you to see why it is paramount that you seek truth from the source that exists beyond the limitations of time and beyond the scope of the sensory realm (the realm where human senses dictate and rule). Psychologically, perception is the process by which we interpret and organize sensation (the feeling we have when one has engaged in an activity) to produce a meaningful experience of the world. Sensation usually refers to the immediate, relatively unprocessed, result of stimulation of sensory receptors in the eyes, ears, nose, tongue, or skin. All five receptors are important in the refining process, the eyes and ears are major, because ultimately, we are motivated by what we see and hear.

Perception better describes one's experience of the world and typically involves further processing of sensory input (mental programming). In practice, sensation and perception are virtually impossible to separate, because they are part of one continuous process. We further see the relationship between senses and perception philosophically. Within the scope of philosophy, perception is defined as achieving knowledge directly through the senses. When you think of senses, you think of feelings. Feelings are relative to how one relates emotionally to an experience or to information. Given the understanding we now have about perception and what influences its formation, we can see why it is important that we identify the debilitating flaws in how we perceive life.

Perceptions may also be defined as how an individual sees people, situations, and life in general. According to this definition, it would be safe to say that parental grooming, personal experiences, peer group influence, media, and social paradigms are key elements involved in our development from birth to present. Our perceptions are not limited to how we view people, situations, and life. It also involves how we view ourselves. Our perceptions are shaped by exterior influences that eventually control and judge us. We accumulate the random principles based on a variety of experiences that possess negative and positive implications. The summation of all these experiences creates what we've embraced as our perception of life. Frankly, these are the ideals that we've chosen to govern our lives. As life progresses, we find that not all of what we've absorbed or perceived as truth is correct.

Perception bridges the gap between people and purpose

What I find most bizarre is that there are individuals who have identified with the fact that though some decisions they made in the past did not work, they continue to nurture these ideals and perform tasks relative to these unprofitable beliefs repeatedly. This, in many circles, is defined as insanity, doing the same things over and over seemingly expecting better results. Here's a valuable piece of advice: wake up! Nothing is going to change except your age. And you will wake up one day when you're much older and look into your mirror and begin to run down a list of "what ifs." Tragic isn't it? This vicious cycle takes place each and every day. So, take some positive steps to break the cycle. When an idea, thought, or philosophy proves to be ineffective and fails to bring about the desired results in your life (results that should promote excellence, growth, and purposeful living), it becomes necessary to reevaluate its value and make the necessary changes.

Trial seasons alert us that we're due an eye examination (a perception check). It is possible to strain your "eye of life," that is, seeing something that is not there. To strain your eye of life is woefully trying to see that which belongs to those who attempt to impose their views on you. You're trying to foresee that which has not been predestined for you on the road toward your purpose. The strain has caused blurred vision. You're blinded to the truth.

Whether nearsighted or farsighted, your vision (perception) is distorted, meaning nothing is as it seems. The challenge is to admit that somewhere along the road of life, *you missed it.* You must acknowledge that you don't have all the answers to life, and what you think you know is in need of modification. It is evident that your philosophy of life just isn't working. I know that this will be a very difficult thing to do. Perhaps you've been preaching it to family and friends all your life with a strong personal conviction.

Important Note: *A strong, passionate conviction concerning a perception (principle or philosophy) does not qualify it as being the truth. Neither does it validate perception as personally nor universally beneficial, profitable, or essential. It is not above scrutiny.*

Come to terms with what is true, and make the proper decisions based on that truth. To do so will change your life. This change will bring you back on the path of destiny's plan. You will discover in our next area of concern that associating and depending on the wrong people will ultimately distort your perception, which will in turn throw you off course with the divine plans and purposes for your life.

The Influence of Purpose (Predetermined Plan)

Where purpose is unknown, abuse is inevitable.
—Myles Monroe

I never knew that there were so many people who didn't have a clue as to where they were headed in life. At first, it was unfathomable, then and then I remembered that there was a time in my life that I, too, didn't have a clue as to where I was in life. Some persons encouraged me to pursue one area of life, while others dictated that a particular area was the only reasonable choice for my life's pursuit. Needless to say, I was torn emotionally, spiritually, and relationally. Who was right and who was wrong? There were personal endeavors that I wanted to pursue. No one suggested any of these. Many times you're caught in life's crossfire and you must choose. One of several choices is made: you may choose to try and please everyone, which is impossible; you may choose the way of the most credible influence in your life; or you may choose to weigh the advice of others as you consult with your inner voice, your divine source. Hopefully, you'll choose the latter.

Unfortunately, an overwhelming majority choose the way of the world (personal and/or societal influences). Again, we see people and society at large shaping the perceptions of those in pursuit of purpose. I personally know an assistant district attorney who spent fifteen years in the field of law and was totally dissatisfied with his life's choice. He was, as many still are, trying to fulfill his parents' expectations of him. Needless to say, he eventually decided to leave the field of law and pursue the area he was passionate about, that of sales and marketing. Since making the change, he expressed that he had never been as happy and as fulfilled in life as he is today.

There are myriad stories like this one that chronicle the fact that people are constantly persuaded into making decisions about their purpose in life that sometimes leave them miserable and unfulfilled. Walking out of step with your true purpose in life can prove to be a critically debilitating issue of life. I have witnessed individuals who have sought comfort or escape from this dilemma by giving in to the lure of substance abuse, breaching of relational commitment, and/or fracturing societal parameters.

Not knowing how to, or where you fit in life creates an innate personal dilemma that could result in abuse in one form or another. Psychiatrists' offices, counseling centers, and spiritual consultants are inundated with individuals who lack an understanding of their purpose. They give in to the abuses that plague our society today. They seek help due to problems caused by personal abuse or a societal violation. In the end, the abuse of life can be directly connected with a void of true purpose. Their lives lack meaning. The common mistakes in the search for meaning are found in our limiting the source, resource, and reach necessary for discovery. The meaning or purpose we are in search of transcends our finite limitations. It is found in the deeper quest, the spiritual quest of self. Your spiritual quest of self is found in and is relative to God, the infinite source, the infinite resource, and the infinite reach—"for in Him we live and move and have our being" (Acts 17:28*a*).

As the earlier years of my life passed, gradually, it dawned on me that as I began my quest toward the why of my life, I was being drawn into a relationship with God. Until that time, God was just a concept I was born and raised to acknowledge. For whatever reason, one day as I was pondering life, which was a usual thing for me to do, I experienced this deep, innate hunger wanting to know for myself the truth about this God of my early childhood. Was he real? And if he was, how did he fit into the scheme of my life? I later discovered that it was not about Him fitting into the scheme of my life but me fitting into the scheme of His being. Somehow, I knew that there was more to Him than just the rituals of religion that I knew as a child. In search of the why of my life, I encountered the source of my life, and as my relationship with him developed, I began to understand who I was and why I was.

As a result of my daily relationship with Him and a constant hunger for His presence, His purpose for my life was revealed. It was then that I understood this truth that had evaded me throughout my youthful life. I came into the knowledge that my life was not my own and that I was given life for His earthly use, whenever and wherever He had predetermined. I understood that the spheres of influence that I was privy to and the opportunities that were available to me were orchestrated by Him. By choice, I became a life partner with God. I knew that successes in my life would be dependent on my decision to make choices about my life according to His will concerning life. There was a sense of peace in that arrangement that overshadowed me, and I've been walking in this realization since then.

Walking out of step with your true purpose in life can prove to be a critical debilitating issue of life

One author expressed it this way: "Think for one moment of what is taking place in the mind of the person who awakens in the morning and realizes, *'Without God, I am nothing; but with God, all the powers of harmony unite in me to express themselves,'* or who ponders some scriptural passage such as, *'He performeth the thing that is appointed for me. ... The Lord will perfect that which concerneth me. ... Whither shall I go from thy spirit? Or whither shall I flee from thy presence? If I make my bed in hell, behold, thou art there. ... Yea, though I walk through the valley of the shadow of death, I will fear no evil: for thou art with me.'* Think of what it means to a businessman, leaving for his office, or a mother, sending her children off to school, to know that they are not alone—wherever they are, the Spirit of God is with them, and where that Spirit of God is, there is liberty."[3]

The above statement opened my spiritual eyes to the existence of an ever-present divine presence and the constant participation of a divine intent and initiative in my life. Therefore, I knew then that my perception of purpose in life would be tainted if I saw it only through the eyes of selfish ambition (whether of my own making or of others). The trial season of life positions us to take a second look at why we are doing what we do in life. This season sharpens our focus and brings clarity to what really is. Let's face facts: we are all pretty good at convincing ourselves of anything we want to do in life, good or bad. The importance of the trial season of life is that it helps us to sort out our mistakes, our bad judgments, and our areas of weakness. We are able to clearly identify and categorize the issues of life. Clearly stated, the light of truth consumes the darkness of life and our crooked paths are revealed. Based on our acceptance, resolve, and properly guided initiatives, they are made straight.

Important Note: *When the light of truth does come on in our lives, we discover that we have tried to meet certain needs in the wrong way. It isn't that the needs are not real; it is just that we have tried to meet these needs in inappropriate ways.*

Knowing your purpose is key to fulfilling the needs in your life. Purpose known equals needs fulfilled. If you try to fill the needs in life with anything other than those elements conducive to purpose, you will find yourself in a state of bedlam. You will find yourself living life under a cloud of question marks. Allow the summer season of hardships/trials to clear the mind and erase the question marks concerning purpose.

3

Impurities Examined: Understanding How Debilitating Issues Operate

The operation of debilitating issues engages many sources. A few of these sources are found in the influence of people and the obsession with habits, possessions, and social status. These and many others contribute to the impurities exposed during the trials of your life. In this chapter, I will emphasize the impact people's influence can have in our lives. Over twenty years I have rendered professional services to people in multiple ways. I am convinced that regardless of which source hampers you, it originated through the influence of someone at a pivotal point in your life. People influence us as to how we should feel about other people, possessions, financial position, careers, romance, and eventually shape our destiny. So this chapter is dedicated to viewing people and how they operate as they sow the seeds that impact how you live out your life. It will not be an exhaustive study but will be practical in examining controlling relationships.

This approach to controlling relationships is in no way intended to repudiate the fact that there are healthy relationships to embrace, and there are people in this world who are truly concerned about our well-being. But, we should take care in knowing who our true friends are. They are not difficult to identify. True friends are selfless. They consistently, at various degrees of expression, celebrate with us as we grow as individuals and advance in life. They cry with us when we are faced with disappointments. When we begin to feel like we just don't measure up, they are there for us. Then, with a sincere heart, they empower us to keep moving ahead. They show us by their caring attitude that life is not about being better than anyone else but, rather, becoming our best selves.

Controlling relationships are unhealthy. They thrive on keeping you in an unprogressive state. In many cases, the individuals you're involved with in unhealthy relationships seek to keep you dependent and feeling inferior to them. They sow seeds in your lives that lead to personal dysfunction, depression, broken dreams, and a host of other debilitating characteristics. So, how do these seeds operate? The seeds that birth and nurture debilitating issues develop similar to that of *creeping paralysis*. These seeds can be identified as seeds of opinion rather than truth, discord rather than harmony, despair rather than hope, and fate rather than destiny. Then, the unnoticeable development of emotional and spiritual debilitation begins. The discourse on the following pages will be a broad stroke of a very involved and complex process. I sincerely hope that you will embrace the gist of this concept anyhow.

To begin, notice the process described as creeping paralysis. Creeping paralysis is the slow and unnoticeable loss of voluntary movement in a part of the human body. This is caused by disease or injury anywhere along the motoneuron path from the brain to the muscle fiber. The individual is unaware of this condition until it has infiltrated a part of the body. As we approach the concept of understanding how our impurities function in us, I will incorporate some important elements of human paralysis that will expand the depth of our understanding as it relates to how debilitating issues operate.

As we progressively move toward the close of our last two chapters of the summer (trial) season, I hope that you have identified and can relate to some of the issues discussed thus far.

I trust that you recognize that the purpose of your trial season must be embraced rather than avoided. This chapter will assist you in understanding the hidden operations and methodical deterioration process of these exposed innate impurities. There are two influences operating in this world: one edifies (builds up) and the other eradicates (tears down).

The impurities exposed represent the eradicating influences we've opened up our lives to and have allowed these impurities to begin a slow invisible process of paralyzing our personal development. As this paralysis continues, it can hinder our forward movement in life. The three elements of paralysis we shall explore and parallel are (1) the loss of movement, (2) the brain (home of the mind, the origin relative to impulse transmission affecting motoneuron response), and (3) the muscle fiber (the destination of the path of motoneuron). As we discuss these elements, you will begin to parallel the relative symptoms that occur when faced with these three elements in your personal life situation.

Paralysis—Loss of Movement

One of the defining characteristics of paralysis is loss of movement. The loss of movement is connected with defective and weakened muscle tissue, debilitated motor activity, and nerve damage. Such conditions limit an individual's ability to participate effectively in the business of life. Likewise, individuals who are frustrated with themselves in the trial season of their lives are aware of their limited progress, successes, and achievements. The exhausting push with no payoff has left them disappointed about life. The restrictions of their participation in life are apparent, and now they feel emotionally, spiritually, and socially handicapped. These unexpected factors prompt individuals to ask themselves questions like: How did this happen to me? When did this happen? And why did this happen? These are the questions that haunt us most during our trial season.

Think about it. One day, we are young, vibrant, and ready

to conquer the world with our brilliant ideas. Then, it is as if we awaken to another life, far from where we began dreaming. Since that time in dreamland, we experience cyclical/revolving periods of the same occurrences in our lives, year in and year out. You may be asking the why questions. A large part of the reason is that our dreams were thwarted, and our progress crippled by the poisonous stings inflicted by unscrutinized opinions of others. These slowly infected what I call our visionary system (motoneuron system). This is our system of motion, because vision stimulates and ignites us to move toward our dreams. When our visionary system is negatively influenced, our enthusiasm diminishes. Our pace in life putters and staggers along until we give up and/or give in.

An important fact about vision, destiny, and progress is that it's not enough to just think or talk about them. They require constant forward motion. The following passage of Scripture implies the mind-set of our divine source concerning purpose and movement, "Run and not be weary, walk and not faint" (Isaiah 40:31). This is a challenge that does not advocate stopping or backward movements. Rather, it promotes a time to move swiftly ahead and another time to tread slowly and carefully but still forward. But, by no means does it suggest that we should stop.

Our pursuit of purpose in life was intended to be a continuous and fervent endeavor. The hidden agenda of the enemies of destiny is to formulate a strategy of attack that will day-by-day, week-by-week, and month-by-month eat away at your dreams and visions. The attack continues until finally, your enthusiasm is almost nonexistent, and the aches and pains of their poisons bring you to a complete stop in life. Ultimately, once you stop, you will begin the process of backward movement. If not corrected, you will regress to an "old state" of existence, which could be even worse than before. Your condition will be worse simply because, emotionally, when an individual gives up on any pursuit in life, their preconditioned mind processes it as a failure. Any suggestion of failure chips away at our wall of confidence, taking just a little bit more of ourselves away from us. Don't let it happen!

True friends are selfless

In an unhealthy relationship, the reasons an individual will level personal attacks toward you may be summed up as follows: Firstly, they're not going anywhere, therefore, they don't want you to go anywhere either. Remember, misery loves company. Secondly, it is impossible to sincerely pursue your purpose in life without acquiring a spirit of excellence. Once acquired, excellence triggers promotion in life (see Daniel 6:1–3). As a result, your pursuit of excellence will shed light on their mediocrity. In unhealthy relationships, the imperatives to their agenda are to pour the water of negativism on the fire of your enthusiasm, to nurture the obstacles that make you question your abilities, and slowly to infect or distort the principles of truth that nurture the muscles of purpose.

The process is simple; it begins with the agent (individual) of paralysis sowing their opinion into your life as a friend. This, of course, will be done under the pretense of being a voice of reason. As time passes, with precision and subtlety, that individual creates a platform, or should I say an influential position in your life. At this point, you will begin to receive unsolicited advice, suggestions, or ideas that will tend to contradict your expressed goals. These contradictions will cause you to question what you know to be true. Spinning webs of illusionary trust, the connection to the vital emotional trapdoors of your life is secured. They now possess the strings that govern your life.

Witchcraft Manipulation
Preston Williams II

Humanity surges with uncontrollable passions
And ungoverned grief; falling prey to the
Master manipulators.

31

Imposing unsolicited, selfish propositions;
They violate. Using persuasive stimuli …
That which is desired most.

Trapping their prey in a web meticulously
Spun for capture, a season of control
And exploitation.

An ego fix for the one,
Misplaced passions and discontentment
For the other …
Bewitched.

This process continues until you lose yourself in what others think of you. You now find yourself in what I call "witchcraft manipulation." This is a condition in which people control you and your destiny. They spend enough time with you to know exactly what buttons to push. They are the sensitive areas of your life that make you tick. Now that you depend on their relationships, the worth of your *being* is tied to their opinion of you. While it is important to understand that God does opt to express Himself (edify, counsel, and empower) to us through individuals, our total dependence and trust should not be in the individuals but in Him. Those with the best intentions can, at times, miss the voice of God concerning your life. After all, they, too, are fallible. So, it is important that you understand how to discern the difference between when someone's approach is edifying and properly corrective versus when the approach is one that has a devaluing, debilitative, and destructive impact on your forward pursuit of purpose.

The Mind (The origin of Transmission)

In paralysis, the origin of impulse transmission effecting motoneuron response is the brain. In theology, the origin of impulse transmission affecting movement toward vision is the mind. The brain is the home/temple of the mind. It is here that we develop opinion, personal philosophy, and beliefs. These beliefs determine how we respond to life. It is in the soil of the mind that debilitating seeds are sown. It has been said that, "He who controls the mind controls your destiny." The mind is the battlefield upon which the war of control is fought. On this battlefield, a mixture of the seeds of truth and fallacy are sown. We are given the opportunity to choose which of the two we will embrace and then we live life through the eyes of its philosophies (good or bad).

The summer trial season exposes us to these seeds of choice. We are told by the patriarchs of old that individuals are transformed by the content of the mind. Hence, we are challenged to renew the mind as the means of personal transformation (Romans 12:2). Basically, we have conformed or have taken the formation of the world's systems and philosophies. If we are to be all that God has predetermined for us to be, it is imperative that we be transformed. To expand this statement, it is imperative that we transcend learned forms or behaviors and begin to open our minds to greater possibilities. That can be accomplished by reprogramming the minds. The question is: From what state are we reprogramming our minds? It is from a state of mental bondage and impoverishment caused by the seeds of contaminated opinion. The state of our mind determines how we move, or don't move, in life. It determines how we maintain our *being* … our evolving self.

James Allen, in his book *As a Man Thinketh,* not only brings clarity to my point but expands it by saying:

> Mind is the master power that molds and makes,
> And man is mind, and evermore he takes
> The tool of thought, and shaping what he wills,
> Brings forth a thousand joys, a thousand ills:—
> He thinks in secret, and it comes to pass:
> Environment is but his looking-glass.[4]

Here we can clearly see that developing a solid understanding of the power of our thoughts will assist us in understanding how motives and ambitions are shaped. If you don't properly nurture your thought-life, you will have impaired perception, distorted beliefs, wrong motives, and selfish ambitions. If we don't leave the sentinel of truth posted in the watchtower of our minds guarding our thoughts, then the enemy of our success will slip into the environment of our thoughts under the cover of obliviousness.

It is at this point that the transmission of debilitating information is sent to affect our walk in life. Amazingly enough, life does require a season of trials to challenge our abilities, test our knowledge or the lack of, and make demands on our beliefs. We need seasons that will prompt us to take a closer look at those we allow to influence our lives. I am still in awe of how much we depend on the affirmation of others, sometimes to the degree of emotional dependence. We must guard our thought-life and discern the voices of influence, whether they be the voice of the edifier or the voice of the contaminator.

All the wisdom of this world is but a tiny raft upon which we must sail when we leave this earth. If only there was a firmer foundation upon which to sail, perhaps some divine word.

—Socrates

The Muscle of Faith (The Path of Transmission)

The cultivated brain transmits the signal that either stimulates movement or discourages movement. The muscles of the body facilitate movement when properly stimulated. Likewise, the muscles of the mind, if properly stimulated, will facilitate movement as well. The muscle of the mind that is relevant to this particular section is *faith*. Faith to endure the trials of life, knowing that all things, good or bad, work toward attracting the best that was predetermined for you before you were even born. The muscle of faith is directly influenced by what seeds we've allowed in the mind (the origin of transmission). If the seeds of thought are edifying, the mind transmits the building blocks of faith, which in turn create the stimuli for action and movement. If the seeds of thought are contaminated, the mind transmits a destructive virus that slowly manipulates the muscle structure of success (faith) and cripples the forward movement of destiny in your life.

I must reiterate the fact that this process is slow. Because of unconsciousness, this destructive and debilitating influence works its way into the faith muscle structure so slowly and so meticulously that as time passes, it is as if the effects become a part of the individual's life, which in turn, is accepted as the norm.

The summer season of trials is so uncomfortable because its purpose is to alert you to a problem that you've accepted as a permanent part of your life. I've heard and read stories of professional athletes playing with dislocated shoulders, broken bones, cracked ribs, and life-threatening conditions. Because of the demands of team members, coaches, and fans, they sometimes never receive the attention needed for proper healing. Eventually, the aches and pains become their norm, and they learn to live with the handicaps. But there comes a time when the advancement of the condition manifests itself. The condition then takes them out of the game permanently. Handicapped and forced to accept that their passion in life has been stripped away, these professional athletes then remember the physician's corrective counsel they rejected during the previous summer seasons. Likewise, individuals live with educational, emotional, spiritual, and social debilitating conditions that have become their norm. Consequently, their passions in life are stripped away, and their life's pursuit comes to a halt. The muscle of faith did not receive proper *seed* maintenance.

The muscle of faith is directly influenced by what seeds we've allowed in the mind

Somewhere along the line, the muscle of faith was weakened into believing the lie about life instead of the truth. Soon, feelings of insignificance, hopelessness, mediocrity, and other internal struggles creep into our thought-life. The impurities that slept silently in the crevices of our lives have been awakened. We find ourselves at the crossroad of decisions that must be made.

Making the critical decisions that affect the progression of life is the culminating purpose of the summer season. We all need a little heat in our lives to prompt us into deciding which road in life to travel. You have two choices at this point. Which will you choose? Curse the summer season for bringing attention to the problem and become disgruntled and disregard the truth—then end up living life in a state of denial? Or, celebrate the summer season that exposed the impurities in time to prevent further debilitation, and embrace the prescribed counsel necessary for healing? Believe it or not, the masses choose to curse the summer season and ignore the exposed impurities. I want to challenge you: dare to be different.

I close with these words by Robert Frost, an American poet (1874–1963) who gave the world this simple yet profound truth:

> Two roads diverged in a wood,
> I took the one less traveled by,
> And that has made all the difference.

4

Impurities Isolated: Restricting Further Contamination

The final stage in the summer season involves isolating the impurities exposed in the previous chapters. Isolating the impurities restricts further contamination. Nearing the end of the natural summer season, the earth's temperature begins to modify as the fall season approaches. The effects of certain parasites on the vegetation and plant life are visible. As was stated in chapter 1, the presence of aphids (debilitating issues) are readily detected by marks, wrinkles, or abnormalities on the plants. When we parallel these effects to our personal experiences, we identify similarities. Being pierced and sucked, we're marked by limited success and marginal happiness, wrinkled with despair and hopelessness, and mentally isolated by abnormalities of insignificance and questionable abilities. Preservation is necessary, and isolation of the problem is, undoubtedly, very essential.

In the natural realm, a number of techniques are utilized in restricting further contamination. One of the techniques used is chemical treatment—fungicides. Fungicides are toxic substances applied to prevent the growth of or to kill fungi detrimental to plants, animals, or humans. Most agricultural fungicides are sprayed or dusted on seeds, leaves, or fruit to prevent the spread of rust, smut, molds, or mildew.

This toxic substance is used to isolate the impurity. Notice that the substance sprayed destroys only the debilitating parasites;

it does not destroy the life of the plant, animal, or human. So, let's make a final parallel to prepare ourselves progressively for the next season in our lives. The toxic agents that we must apply in life to isolate the effects of debilitating issues are our *refined will*, mixed with the *application of truth*. This is a lethal combination to the parasites that affect personal growth and success in life.

Philosophically and psychologically speaking, "will" is the capacity to choose among alternative courses of action and to act on the choice made. Your will is particularly in noticeable form when the action of *choosing* is directed toward a specific goal or is governed by definite ideals and principles of conduct. *Willed* behavior contrasts with behavior stemming from instinct, impulse, reflex, or habit. None of these involves conscious choice among alternatives. Willed behavior contrasts also with the vacillations manifested by alternating choices among conflicting alternatives.[5] This is when an individual is indecisive, wavering from one course of action or opinion to another. This type of person will never make any progress. Why? No action.

As you may have noticed, will and application go hand in hand. They are the explosive distinguishing features of what I consider as "living life" versus "life living you!" Having the capacity to choose among alternative courses of action, and acting on that capacity, are two totally independent issues. One can have the capacity to choose and yet not act on it. Another may act on the capacity without the benefit of truth as the substance of that capacity and end up in the same dilemma … dead end.

Will is the capacity to choose among alternative courses of action and to act on the choice made

This is the foundation of my reasoning that they are separate, yet equally important issues. The key to isolating further contamination of debilitating issues is to make purpose-driven decisions with a refined will based on the application of truth. When these two equally important agents combine, they set off a lethal effect in your present situation. The effect is … *change*! This is more than just merely a word. Change is your movement toward destiny. Change is the reformation of your attitude concerning your present situation. Change is the movement that places you back in line with destiny's original intent. Change based on truth constricts the flow of error and repairs the breaches of the past. Change prepares an individual for success, creating an innate sense of flexibility toward life's pursuits. Change, my friend, is one of few things in life that has stood the test of time, and has remained a constant phenomenon.

My professional secular career endeavors led me to the IBM Corporation. One of the most interesting things I noticed was their slogan, "The only constant in life is change." Unfortunately for IBM, that slogan came a day late and billions of dollars short. IBM carved their place in the history of business enterprise as a leader in mainframe computers in the last few decades of the twentieth century. The dilemma was that they couldn't fathom a computer in every home in America. After all, who could afford such a thing? Well we all know the ending to that story, and the name of the main character is Bill Gates.

I believe that there is a danger in riding on the successes of the past. What made life happy, content, and prosperous yesteryear may not be an effective way to function today. Comfortability and complacency are the main enemies to change. They present a viable threat to your future success and personal growth. To better understand change let's further explore the power of a refined will.

A Refined Will—Its Power

A refined will based on truth tends to bring pause to unhealthy relationships and hasty or unsound decisions. There is a pause, because now, you're rethinking your methods of operation due to the warring concepts now existing within you. Your comfort zones are now challenged by the broader parameters of your newly enlightened possibilities. Some friends will applaud the revitalized you, while others will turn up their "I'm OK, you're OK" noses in the air and revile the new you. Let me go on the record here and say, just because your situation in life is "OK" doesn't necessarily mean that it is right or nurturing for you. It may just mean that you've chosen fate that is settling for what your contaminated will chooses to believe. The will that has been shaped by the very relationships and propaganda you've come to accept as an important constant in your life. Settling is not an option for destiny seekers. Therefore, a refined, balanced will is a prerequisite for forward movement.

Important Note: *Because things are "OK" doesn't necessarily mean that it is right or nurturing for you. It may just mean that you've chosen fate that is settling for what your contaminated will chooses to believe.*

I'd like to focus on four manifestations of what I consider to be the refined will. They are stated with the supposition that truth is the foundation by which you now govern your life. Therefore, the refined will is manifested by

- intentionally focusing of one's attention on relative goals (short term and long term) and rethinking questionable standards and principles of conduct;
- scrutinizing all options before responding and then respond confidently because of the assurance that it is the best course of action to take as it relates to destiny;
- the ability to just say no to any person or practices that cause a potential distraction or threatens the principles that now govern your walk toward your best self;
- finally, perseverance in the face of obstacles and frustrations while pursuing your goals. When faced

with the difficulties of life, remember to just … stand firm! Turn your stumbling blocks into stepping-stones.

These four manifestations of the refined will should be the mission statement of any individual who has experienced the fiery summer season of life and has come to terms with what must be done. It becomes one's "charge to keep." Nothing is more exciting than to witness a rejuvenated mind and a confident, steadfast will illuminated by truth. No matter what challenges an individual is faced with, once light illuminates and invades the perimeter of that challenge, a peace saturates the soul of that person even before a solution is offered. It is the peace that resolves the question of why. Once the why is made known, half the battle and struggle of the summer season is over. You're left only with the "how" of resolution. Before moving on to the how, I must stress that your will must be resolute and fixed on the fact that change is a prerequisite, and that no matter what problem area of your life is revealed, you will give it its due attention. This may require modifying the situation or a complete detachment from the area of concern. Indeed, only a stern will is capable of weathering the storm of life while changes and modifications are in progress.

Growing up, in my early teenage years and even as a young adult, I would often wonder what people meant when they described an individual as being "strong willed." From the tone of their conversation, it was as if having a strong will was a character flaw of sorts. I later discovered what they really were implying. In their mind, the strong-willed individual was one who could not be swayed by their counsel or their hidden agendas. That infuriated those people who would want the individual to do as they say but was unsuccessful. Hence, that person was negatively labeled strong willed.

I've come to appreciate the characteristic of being strong willed. To me, that is an individual who is confident in what one knows. Such a person will not allow any form of distraction or influence to rock his world of beliefs. One writer describes it as being, "steadfast and unmovable" (1 Corinthians 15:58). Another describes it as, "not being tossed to and fro" (Ephesians 4:14). Of course, I must say that a strong will based on truth versus that of error manifests extremely different results. Therefore, having a strong will in and of itself is not a flaw. It is important to note that how a strong will is nurtured will distinguish its operation in life.

Application of Truth

This section focuses primarily on the illumined mind. This mind is willing to open up itself to the dynamics of truth. If you will keep an open mind to the principles involved in each of the four sections and begin to apply the principle nuggets in your life, you will find that the results are nothing short of awesome and fulfilling on different levels. The key word and most damaging part of this thought is "if." I've been involved in people-oriented professions for over twenty years, in fact, all of my adult life. I spent a considerable amount of my time in secular careers with companies such as IBM, American Express, and Budget Rent-A-Car Corporation, to name a few. My education, personal experiences, and most important, my relationship with God positioned me for accelerated promotions in the areas of sales and marketing management. In the religious sector, my areas of service included pastoral leadership, counselor, and presently, educator. Exposure to both the secular and the religious arenas placed me directly in the center of observing, training, influencing, and shaping people for success. Experiencing both realms created a sense of balance necessary for truly assisting all kinds of people with different stations in life.

The common problem I encountered in both professional services was the overwhelming lack of what I consider to be *key principle application*. The success or failure of any individual is found in the issue of commitment to proper application of key principles. The proper application of truth is vital to the seasons that will follow your summer (trial) season. As was aforementioned, a renewed will gives you the wherewithal to make changes, but the application of truth principles provides the path to change. God, the source of life, revealed himself as the word of truth. The word was placed in form (flesh) and dwelt among mankind to bring about spiritual, social, economic, and political change, but more important, to reconnect us with God, the source of abundant life. Christ (the Word), pointed us in the proper path for our renewed will. He said, "I am the Way, the truth, and the life" (John 14:5). Undeniably, he is the only way (path), the only truth (principle), and the only life (provisions and potential).

This way (path), truth (principle), and life (provisions and potential) places those of us searching for consistent development through each season in a newfound awareness of an eternal realm, where the only limitations that exist are those we allow to contaminate and debilitate us. Truth will stimulate us to look and live beyond questionable worldly influences and limitations. The application of truth will trigger an untapped dimension within us to begin living life at its maximum potential on the earth, knowing that the personal development God has begun in us during the summer (trial) season, He will complete. As we, through the acceptance of truth, tap into this new dimension, all the power of harmony will be evoked within us. We will triumphantly and effectively live life in a state of peace that will pass all understanding.

Here is a final thought before proceeding to section 2. You're about to approach a new season in your life. The summer season is concluding. You have been exposed to some issues that are critical to your personal and spiritual development. Everything that you've experienced up to this point in your life has been placed in the balance of God's intended purpose for your existence here on earth. You've weighed and scrutinized many areas of concern that represent your comfort zones. Now you are faced with some uncomfortable but much-needed decisions you must make. This is your pivotal moment, a moment that will define the rest of your life. The summer season has forced you to acknowledge your personal limitations. You've exhausted the finite possibilities, but you have discovered your way out and the assistance you'll need to make the necessary changes.

The success or failure of any individual is found in the issue of commitment to proper application of key principles

Truth is your knight in shining amour, guiding your way through the wilderness of life, leading you toward the infinite source and the limitless possibilities that belong to you in your pursuit of purpose. Once truth is applied, your path will be made straight and your successes in life are certain. Please remember that progress and success come with a price.

After the summer (trial) season comes the fall (release) season. This is where the price is brought into clearer focus and initiated. It is a time to test the renewed will. Progression, prosperity, and peace of mind mandate the fulfillment of this season in your life. The exposed impurities and contaminated areas of your life are dealt with in this season. Let me restate, it is not enough to be aware of the hindrances and issues in our lives. We must isolate them to prevent further contamination. Clearly, it is also not enough to be aware of and to isolate the hindrances and issues in life. We must deal with them in the corrective arena of truth. Truth will require you to be proactive in your approach during the fall (release) season. So, don't resist what must be done. Prolonging decision making, and the corrective actions essential to your well-being, will only intensify the dilemma you're experiencing.

Every person who has known dissatisfaction, hopelessness, emptiness, and frustration will some day have to face the purpose of their summer (trial) season. The best of individuals find themselves heavily challenged when faced with the unknown of this season. They go through life unaware of the fact that there is a missing link in their chain of harmonious living until that pivotal moment when the light of truth illuminates the darkness of their disillusionment. It is important that we not let an hour of any day go by without consciously reminding ourselves that the goal of life is to possess a mind developed by truth. Having internalized this goal, we will consistently press forward to attain it.

It is my hope that you take the principles set forth in this book and appropriate them in your daily life. Review the chapters repeatedly to determine the season in which you are presently operating, and apply the principles that are relevant to your situation. There are very few things in life that I am certain of, this I am certain of beyond the shadow of a doubt; it is possible for anyone to change the trend of their life and thus affect the circumstances of life's journey. Change comes not solely by hearing or reading truth but by making it an active part of your daily experience. Do it until it consumes every moment of the day. It should not be just an occasional thought. The finest hours of your life are ahead of you. Don't look back, keep moving forward and enjoy the refining process; it is for your benefit. Having said that, prepare yourself as you enter into the next realm of personal development and discovery in your seasons of destiny's perfection.

Illumination dissolves all material ties and binds men
together with the
Golden chains of spiritual understanding; it acknowledges
only the leadership
of the Christ; it has no ritual or rule but the divine, impersonal
Universal Love; no other worship than the inner Flame
that is ever lit at

the shrine of Spirit. This union is the free state
of spiritual brotherhood.
The only restraint is the discipline of Soul, therefore we know liberty
without license; we are a united universe without physical limits;
a divine service to God without ceremony or creed.
The illumined walk
without fear—by Grace.

—The Infinite Way

PART II
Fall: The Season of Change

Is it fitting to consider what is impermanent, painful, and subject to change as, "This is mine, this am I, this is my self"?

—Pali Tripitaka

5
The Coolness of Fall:
The Climate for Personal Change

Life: Chapter Two
Preston Williams II

In life, time passes from one stage to another;
Embrace it, don't chase it. Let love develop experience
And grow further. We understand not fully who we are,
Still less what we might be; yet in our hearts spiritual wisdom
Cries out ... "Be patient, seek Me and I'll set you free."

Life chapter one seems like words and music that can't
Quite become a song; so we cry and sigh then we
Try again ... with perseverance and faith we
Right what went wrong. Not every thought can find
Its words, not all within is known; for minds and
Hearts have many chords that never yield their tone.

Tastes, instincts, feelings, passions and powers sleep there,
Unfelt and unseen; our new lives lie hidden in our old ones ...
The lives that should have been. Affections who's transforming
Force could mold the heart anew; strong purpose, pure motives
That could change the course of all we think and do; lie
dormant

Within us till we turn over the pages of life and
begin chapter two.

("What the caterpillar calls the end of the world,
God calls a butterfly.")

One morning, I sat on the fence in our front yard like I had
done many times before; I suddenly realized the calmness in the
atmosphere. Summer was coming to a close. The once hot, high-
noon sun had transitioned into a coolness that brought ease to
the earth's scorched surface. My daily assigned chores that before
seemed so tedious and drudgery were now less taxing because
of the changing season. Soon, the trees would shed their leaves,
detaching themselves from the source that once nurtured their
existence. I was seventeen then, and I was experiencing a principle
of nature that would one day make a profound impact on my
adult life. So much of my life was ahead of me; I could never
have seen the many challenges that would confront me. Later,
I would become the main character in God's unique love story
concerning my personal development.

As a young adult, like nature, I was going through some
changes in my life. The trees had begun shedding their leaves.
I, too, was releasing some people, things, and ideals I once held
close in my life. Years later, I have come to realize that this is
an ongoing cycle; it is life's process of growth and renewal. I
appreciate my childhood and the unique experiences that only a
small town could humbly offer. In retrospect, I ponder the subtle
lessons nature has taught me. The lesson was the importance and
the certainty of the constant challenges involved with change.

The calm atmosphere and the shift of the earth's temperature
after the summer months was God's way of initiating the cool-
down period necessary for the vegetation to begin a new process.
This was the earth's beginning stages of *cleansing*. The earth was
shedding that which the summer heat had exposed and that
which was infected by the impurities that flourished in the heat

of summer season. Nature was turning the last page in the chapter of another year's summer and introducing the first page of the next chapter in life's seasonal process. Nature was again yielding herself to the caring providential hand of God, its source.

Nature has one up on humanity in this area. Nature instinctively yields to the perfecting process. Humanity, on the other hand, must make a choice to yield to the perfecting process of change. The principle *choice* will be discussed in more detail in the chapters to follow. One thing I know to be true about change is that it is always accompanied by the appropriate climate. There is a time and a season that is appropriate to approach certain issues in life. There is also a time when one should refrain from, or patiently wait to deal with, certain issues. I accepted this sound advice for a long time, and it was reinforced during my counseling studies. It is, "Never make a decision when you're angry, and never discuss case-sensitive topics when emotions are intense or heightened." There needs to be a cool-down period. This is a time when you enter into the calm of proper reasoning. During this time, you sort through that which must be expressed or initiated.

Coming out of your summer season, you should have come to terms with some realities. By now, the most important of those is the fact that you must modify critical areas in your life. They include your habits, perceptions, friendships, and reason for living. Ironically, the words "fall" and "autumn" are used interchangeably to refer to the season immediately following the summer season. No other season has a dual classification like the fall/autumn season. This is a very unique and interesting fact. My parallel to this season will embrace both identifications. Two major characteristics are connected to each classification. I interpret them as follows. "Autumn" describes the modifications/ change in the climate and the colors of the leaves of plants and trees. "Fall" is simply the release, or falling away, of the leaves affected by summer's infestation. The climate is right and change is inevitable. Based on my personal experience in dealing with major life changes and those garnered through my interventions professionally, I will include in part 2 some of the variables that I deem recurring elements of change. But for now, let's focus on the cool-down process of the fall season.

Humanity ... must make a choice to yield to the perfecting process of change

This cool-down process is of utmost importance. It is a time and a season when you reflectively examine the exposed areas of your life, the areas that are in need of modification. The summer season of trials is history. Take advantage of the enlightened, educational moments, pause to evaluate what and who will be affected in the fall season of change. It is essential that the changes made reflect those areas of our lives that were exposed during the summer. Change is a prerequisite for our successful transition as we progress to the next level of life. Doing so will enhance performance and increase the quality of our emotional, social, spiritual, and provisional well-being. The fall climate affirms the saying "cooler heads prevail." Remember, any decision made in haste or in a time of heated reasoning is a bad decision. Why? It is made without the benefit of calm reasoning and the influence of truth. A hasty decision is usually a decision based on external or internal elements affecting your emotions. The cool ambiance of fall/autumn gives way to personal resolve and to proper application of what has been learned during the season of trial and error.

From my experience, I can say that journalizing your thoughts and applying the many lessons learned throughout life are very therapeutic. Journalizing can be useful in recording valuable insights that will assist you in charting your new course. As the cool-down season continues, use your newfound insights to deal with critical issues such as perceptions, relationships, authoritative figures, debilitating habits, decision making, your pace versus God's pace in life, time management, strong temptation, and spiritual and social adventures. Maintenance of mental and physical needs must also get attention. The climate of fall allows for pause to some situations in life where you question and take note on which practices worked well and which ones did not. Ask yourself this question based on the truth revealed about me and my situation: "What can I do differently?" Don't answer too quickly. Take your time to think this through.

I mentioned in the beginning chapters that the biggest problem today is that some people refuse to take the time to think deeply about life. To ponder life is to have more than a general interest in the daily routine. I firmly believe that it is our responsibility as good stewards of life to pursue it in the spirit of excellence. Excellence is accomplished when you pay attention to the details of your life and make the adjustments necessary for personal growth. When personal growth is achieved, promotion in life and the fulfillment of your higher purpose in this world is inevitable.

The fall/autumn season is the time in your life when destiny summons you into the shade of reason to reflect, renew, and release. The fall weather has a tendency to be more stable at this time of year. Stability of the climate usually affects the mental and spiritual well-being of an individual in a good way. Growing up in southeast Georgia, I usually anticipated the ease that was ushered in with the calmer atmospheric shift and seasonal temperature change. Life seemed more manageable, and the anxieties felt during the summer months subsided into a more relaxed state of mind.

Comparatively, God, the source of life, blows His cool breath into our fall/autumn season, cooling the burning ambers of our minds and awakening us to a new day. It is a second chance of sorts, a chance to right what went wrong, a chance to approach life in the realm of a changed perception interpreted through the eyes of truth. God's direction, protection, and provision are guaranteed in this approach as you sojourn your new path in the perfecting process.

Change is a prerequisite for our successful transition as we progress to the next level of life

Another important aspect of fall's atmospheric change is that the temperatures are cool and pleasant for observers at the telescope. The skies are generally clearer, allowing the observer to look into the night sky amid the darkness and see things that are not so visible in the summer skies. To parallel this metaphorically speaking, from a human perspective, it is the cooled out and poised innate temperament (not temperature) that allows us to clearly observe the night skies of our life. We see that which was not as visible in the heat of our summer (trial) season. The angry, bitter, and frustrated heart might have clouded our perspective, impaired our vision, and kept us from seeing the tangible problems that hindered our progress in life.

Chapter 6 will highlight and deal with identifying these hindrances and suggest methods of implementing practical, necessary courses of action. Change implies *modification* and/or *detachment*. In Mother Earth's process, these are referred to as *pruning* and *rooting up*. Paralleling and distinguishing between the two, we see that *pruning* is to *modifying* as *rooting up* is to *detaching*. While at Camden County High School as a teenager, I did landscaping in a work-study program. Later on at college, I actually worked in this area to earn extra income. This knowledge has helped with understanding these processes and how they benefit the plant life.

The pruning process involves the removal of parts of the woody plants, usually branches or branch tips. This process is performed to achieve several purposes. Namely, to relieve the burden on the remaining parts of the plant, cut out diseased or broken parts, increase the quantity and quality of flowers or fruits, and train individual parts into positions structurally favorable to the health of the plant. One could almost envision how this process favors human life as well. Fall is a season God has allowed in our personal lives to maintain relationships, modify habits, and relieve the burdens exposed in our lives during the summer season. Additionally, pruning our lives increases the abundance that is intended for us and also increases the quality of our lives.

Pruning is also a training process. It trains individual parts into structurally favorable positions. Speaking of relationships, I prefer to use the term orientation rather than train. Why? I don't believe one should train an individual in a relationship but there is an orientation process that takes place within a relationship. Orientation provides opportunity for one to share relational positions with individual acquaintances. This fosters decision as to whether or not the growth of a healthy friendship is possible. On the other hand, "train" to me implies that I am imposing my values on those I presently consider to be my friends as well as prospective ones. If the individual does not approve of your orientation (sharing your relational position ... your likes and dislikes), then pruning will not be the change you'd want to initiate. It would prove to be an ineffective and prolonged problem. Having read the first section of this book, I'm sure that by now you have begun to evaluate your current relationships to determine if you've fallen prey to this unique, yet common esoteric enslavement.

Your personal habits must be retrained. Retraining personal habits is the process of tempering one's innate will to adjust according to a set of standards that contradict the normal mode of operation. In this respect, pruning will take on an act of voluntary submission on the part of the primary individual who seeks change. This will open up to another standard and/or principle for the purpose of growth and personal well-being. In part 1, we discovered that habits are the product of our perceptions, and our perceptions are the product of the collective information we've passionately embraced from all sources we deem credible. Retraining our habits will then involve the reprogramming of our mind. In essence, during the fall season of pruning, we will have to rethink our theology and philosophy of life. It is here that we must decide if modification or detachment is the proper course of action to take.

Pruning is a training process. It trains individual parts into structurally favorable positions

This brings us to our next parallel, rooting up. Unlike pruning, the next level of change is more intense. It is the process of rooting up; this is a total separation from or the denouncing of someone or something as a resolve to making change. Relative to relationships and habits, there are instances where modification will not be an effective option to progressive change in your life. If there is unwillingness to reverse the negative effects or influences imposed upon your life, more drastic means will need to be employed.

The root, in a plant's life, is the channel of water, oxygen, and nutrients; it is the channel of life for the plant. If you want to end the life of a plant, just pull it up by the roots. The parallel of this concept to your life is obvious and should be taken quite seriously. There are some areas of your life that you need to pull up by the roots! Negative people and unfruitful habits have stunted your growth. The summer heat has beaten down upon their shallow influences, and the coolness of the fall has poised you for a moment of evaluation and correction. The life that they imposed upon you in the past was not one of progress and personal well-being. Have you ever considered that maybe you have not moved further along in life because your life reflects that of your friends or confidants? These are individuals that, by association, affirm the acceptance of particular habits in your life that are obviously detrimental to your future welfare. Those who were not so obvious have been exposed during your summer (trial) season for you to specifically deal with in the fall of your life. Now is the time, as one writer says, to, "throw off everything that hinders, and the sin that so easily entangles" (Hebrews 12:1 NIV). What a powerful challenge! Fall is the season to initiate the processes of change so that you may enter within the corridors of a new realm of living.

While I was a first-year student at Lee University in the mid-1980s, I was thirsty for clear direction, accurate counsel, and life-changing impartation. Pastor Joe Edwards, then senior pastor of the North Cleveland Church of God, strongly impacted my life. I was intrigued by his enthusiasm for life and his vocation of ministry. One day I requested a meeting with him, and my request was granted. My sole purpose was to spend some time with this man I admired, and in some ways, emulated. As I entered Pastor Edwards's office, he extended his hand and, with a firm grip, shook my hand. We sat down and began to converse about Sunday's service. After a few moments elapsed, he inquired as to the nature of my visit. I slid forward in my chair and simply asked, "Pastor Edwards, what is the key to your unusual sense of confidence and personal success?" He sat back in his chair, and he smiled at me. For a few seconds, there was silence. Then he returned to a forward position in his chair. With a voice of meekness and wisdom, he said, "Love God and submit to his corrective Word, learn to laugh at yourself, don't take life too seriously, and choose your friends carefully." He continued, "As far as my success, if you want to excel to higher heights, you must first expose yourself to higher heights!" Those words, "expose yourself to higher heights," to me, meant that I had to open myself up to change and be willing to extend beyond my comfort zones. I left his office that day with a sense of profound direction, and my life has never been the same. Mentally and emotionally, I was challenged to make some much-needed changes. The climate of my life was shifting, and God was watching.

Retraining our habits will involve the reprogramming of our mind

For many of you, the climate that you're now experiencing has created an atmosphere conducive for these much-needed changes. The only obstacle that lies in the way of you, your personal growth, and your emotional freedom is your *will* to make the necessary changes that destiny has orchestrated for your benefit. The season has shifted, the time has come, and now the rest is up to you.

The critical decisions to be made will not be easy. Fall season is not only a time of anticipated hope but also a time of indecisive slumber. Summer ended with a sense of hope and anticipation for what was approaching, for something different, anything other than the existing experiences. Indecisive slumber is activated when one is confronted with the unpleasant responsibility of change. The feelings of reluctance, inhibition, and paralyzing anxiety are the result of fear of the unknown. You may begin to question the necessity of change in certain areas that have been exposed. It's difficult to make the decision to modify the people, perceptions, and habits that are regarded as commonplace. So initially, the process of change will be slow paced in some of your more case-sensitive areas. You will probably opt to begin with the less-sensitive areas. By experience, I know that getting over with the more serious areas of need is of greater benefit in the long run. So before you yield to the temptation of getting over with the lesser issues, think carefully, be wise, and tackle those serious ones, which require greater effort and greater sacrifice but in the end reap greater reward.

The longer you put off dealing with those important areas of needed change, the harder it will be to face them. To properly approach your season of change, you must come to a healthy sense of brokenness (innate flexibility to positive influence) and an awareness of unhealthy personal vulnerability. This vulnerability is what others use to control you in relationships; it is the source of comfort zone conditioning. A healthy sense of brokenness is realized at the point of submission of your will to the meticulous shaping of truth. Your personal area of vulnerability is whatever presents the most challenge in the decision-making season of change. Dealing with vulnerability is challenging, because it sometimes requires you to confront controlling parents, associates, previous abusers, and the negative influence of others.

Your past associates know your vulnerabilities and exactly what buttons to push to manipulate situations that surround you and their relationship with you. What was once uncomfortable has now become the norm. The pain and anger these individuals have brought into your life has come to be expected, and change is seen as a peril rather than a path toward personal enrichment. As an escape, you begin to procrastinate and take the indecisive path so as not to disturb your norm. I have one word of advice for you: *don't*! Don't give in to procrastination and indecisiveness.

A final word as I close this chapter. As you move forward during the seasons that are necessary for change in your life, please seek out someone who is qualified to be an accountability source. The missing link in most of our lives is accountability. Not many of us have qualified persons to whom we are answerable concerning key areas of our lives. People to whom we have given permission to ask the hard questions regarding the goals we set and the standards established in truth. In my counseling sessions, I often inform individuals that accountability goes far beyond mere counsel or personal fellowship. It requires answers to the questions, sometimes hard questions. As you matriculate through the seasons of perfection, let me challenge you to fill in this missing link in your life. It may be the component that enables you to synchronize your behavior with your newfound beliefs and the stabilizer that keeps you from spinning out of control and landing back into the misguided control of other influences.

One of my favorite lecturers, Vance Havner, said this about change, "We are challenged these days, but not changed; convicted, but not converted. We hear, but do nothing, and thereby, we deceive ourselves." I believe this to be the prevalent attitude of our day and the consequence of not following through with what we know to be true. I call it the song of a neglected soul. Don't let this be the melody of your life.

6

Dealing With the Season of Indecision

The issues of summer are brought to a silent whisper as we give in to autumn's hypnotic grace. It has not yet occurred to us that the beauty and ease we now enjoy is all a part of the process of change and that during autumn, fall is the other side of this dual-descriptive season. It is the seasonal point of separation. What now seems so perfect will soon matriculate into the next level of transformation. This transformation will result in further discoloration and eventual detachment of the leaves from the tree. For nature, the process is natural and automatic; but for humanity, beings of choice, we are left to decide for ourselves what and/or who will stay in our lives and what and/or who will need to go. This process, if not properly guided, could be disastrous.

In this chapter, I will discuss what happens during this stage before change is initiated. Without speaking in absolute or exhaustive terms, my objective is to make my readers aware that one of the most unproductive moments in any individual's life is *indecision*. I will highlight a few of the manipulative thoughts that tend to romance your reasoning into a state of indecision and emotional slumber. The uncultivated mind overflows with creative excuses in order to avoid anything that has not been programmed as "routine function." Routine function is akin to a built-in protective operation of the mind. This protective operation of the mind will serve you well once you've gone through the renewal process. Then it will be protecting that which benefits the continuum of your well-being versus protecting the negative, contaminated thoughts and perceptions that presently govern your routine way of life.

The Caution of Calm and the Purpose of Ease

The beautiful changing leaves during autumn are quite colorful. So much so, it is very easy for anyone to become mesmerized. Life experiences are not much different. You, too, can be wooed into complacency by the ease and temporary beauty following the heat of the trial summer season. What was exposed to us has now taken on a different color, attitude, poise, and approach. Our circumstances appear to be better; unfortunately, that is exactly what it is, only appearance. You, the decision maker, could be disillusioned and wooed by the temporary adjustments. The question you must ask yourself about the pending issue or the individual representing the source of questionable influence in your life is: Has the situation or person legitimately changed or, am I face to face with a maintenance measure whose sole purpose is to keep me from "pruning" or "clipping"?

Whatever the situation may be, make no mistake, the problem is still there. Previously, you may not have been aware of the situations that are now in your face, probably because at that time they posed no apparent threat. Since your trial season, they were brought to your attention because of their existence, present negative effect, and potential threat. If the proper changes are not initiated, these issues will ultimately go back into hiding, further contaminating, indoctrinating, and nurturing procrastination, thus retarding positive change in your life.

With a keen eye, take the time to look beyond the temporary beauty and embrace the calm of innate reasoning tempered by truth. Acknowledge the guidance of truth and lean not to your own understanding (Proverbs 3:5–6). Without the benefit of truth, there have been limitations to your understanding. These limitations have caused you to be misguided in the past. Don't allow this to perpetuate your ritual or routine functioning as you move toward your future. The past cannot be changed, but it can be understood. As you seek to understand the wisdom you've gained from your experiences, know that all things, whether good or bad, have an ultimate purpose and benefit in your whole life (Romans 8:28). In life, it is easy to overlook the exposed areas that need attention. For the most part, I believe overlooking the reason is so easy due to the fear of change or fear of the unknown.

The Spirit of Fear and Its Fruit: Hesitancy

Fear is an emotion caused by threat of some form of harm, sometimes manifested in bravado or symptoms of anxiety, prompting a decision to fight the threat or escape from it. The threat or harm is usually aimed at the people, objects of affection, and perceptions we've embraced. In this case, the threat is leveled toward those who have caused us to develop a sense of tolerance for mediocrity, abuse, dashed dreams, and anything that disrupts our true course in life. Fear will cause us to either fight the necessary changes or escape them by ignoring the signs. Fear and hesitancy will grip your heart at the procession of this season of calm. Fear paralyzes our intent to change, causing the hesitancy of making the decisions that will be life altering. Yes, fear is an element of our human existence. It is not, however, an unconquerable emotion; fear is controllable. Someone once said, "There is nothing to fear but fear itself." I believe that.

**Courage is not the absence of fear;
it is the presence of fear under control
as one moves forward.**

William Shakespeare, through the voice of Macbeth, gives a glimpse of the ultimate effects of fear if not brought under control by speaking to it. We must affirm that, "Our fears do make us traitors." We may ask, traitors to what? We become traitors to our dreams, our true selves, and our destiny (the reason for having life). Fear is entertained in the mind and heart of individuals because of the unknown. You're not sure how you will survive without that object of affection (that person or perception in your life that has always dominated). There is an uncertainty of how the void will be filled once that person or thing is extracted from your life. Dubious thoughts emerge about how people will respond to you now that certain changes have been enforced. There are a host of other thoughts that will permeate your mind because of fear. The key is to control your fear, harness its negative energy, and convert it into the fuel required to move forward.

On the HBO special *Tyson*, there was a pivotal moment in the movie as Mike Tyson approached his first fight that further illuminates our understanding of fear. At the beginning of Tyson's heavyweight boxing career, he, too, battled with fear. His manager and trainer corrected this debilitating emotion by challenging him with these words, "The difference between a coward and a champion is what each individual does with his fear." Fear is common in every person. What makes one individual ascend to the height of accomplishment while another tumbles to the depths of failure is how each manages their fears. But is fear merely an emotion? I don't think so. As one who embraces a balance between philosophy, psychology, and theology, I contend that fear is not just an emotion. I believe that fear is a spirit (2 Timothy 1:7*a*) that influences our emotions! Its negative influence affects our human spirits, thereby stimulating our emotions to respond accordingly (negative outlook, inhibition toward necessary actions, and faithless professions).

The Bible tells us that God, our source, "has not given us the spirit of fear, but of power, of love, and of a sound mind" (2 Timothy 1:7*b*). This is the spirit and the mind-set we're to operate in during our season of change. When we flow in a God-influenced realm, we open ourselves up to the Spirit, power, love, and infinite mind of God. He is our hope and source of change. We cannot do it alone. The issues in our lives are too deep, too influential, and too personal for us to handle with our own strength. We must come to terms with healthy appreciation for a higher deity who involves himself in our journey through life.

With this in mind, we should travel the roads of life with such an assurance of success that we make the needed changes with minimum resistance. The source of our destiny abides with us through the entire process. He really does care about the minute details of our lives. Here are two questions to consider at this point: Do we really want what God has for us? And if so, are we willing to do what it takes to acquire it? Think about it.

The Birthing of Excuses

There are many who cherish the hope of not having to deal with the difficult issues that plague their future welfare. These individuals hope that things may just work themselves out or, better yet, just go away. Deep within, they doubt their capacity to change. The thought of changing scares them. Soon, the sower of life's discord will begin planting a lethal seed that eventually gives birth to the fruit of not only fear and hesitancy but also excuses. What are excuses? Apart from the general definition given, I invite you to consider to the following seven-point set of expanded definitions. Excuses are:

- responses to natural or spiritual pressure to gain relief from obligations or consequences;
- usually birthed out of comfort zone conditioning (you feel like you're going to lose something of importance);
- negative responses magnifying your weaknesses rather than your strengths;

- cowardly ways of surrendering to adversities;
- the fuel for self-fulfilling adversities—"Death and life are in the power of the tongue" (Proverbs 18:21*a*);
- thieves who rob my tongue of professing assurance, confidence, and faith;
- the greatest enemies to success.

After viewing these additional definitions, it should be quite apparent that immediate attention be given to the subtlety of the excuse trap. Beware of it lest the intuitive response to yield to indecision and stall the necessary changes overtakes you. In this case, you will be robbed of personal development. It is here that one must draw from strength beyond one's limited ability. It is the source of life that must be allowed to flow through, around, in, and from us as we approach these challenges in life. If we do so, we find ourselves transcending petty issues, troubling influences, and hindrances that we depended on so exclusively in the past. We are then able to transcend only because we have come full circle in our lives with what is true. We now embrace God, our true source of change and significance.

Given awareness of the unfruitful influences exposed during our summer season, and the wisdom imparted to us through the voice of truth, we discover that our innate capacity has expanded. Now, the possibility of change is not a "can we?" issue but, rather, a "will we?" Because of the exposure of both issue and solution, it is now clearly a matter of personal choice.

Nothing is as exhausting as indecision, and nothing is so futile

To be indecisive is to be caught between two opinions and be bombarded with uncertainty as to which one to choose. It is to wrestle with what you're accustomed to and that which is newly presented as an alternative to the past. It is the precipitator of imbalance in major areas of your life. In the Epistle of James, the writer considers this to be a psychological condition referred to as "double-mindedness." According to his valuation of indecision, he contends that, "A double-minded individual is unstable in all areas of life" (James 1:8).

The Crossroads of Decision

The crossroads in life demand a decisive response and require the acceptance of personal responsibility for the choices made. I admit that change and decision making are not easy. On the one hand, you find yourself finally at the point of acceptance about the critical areas of your life that require special attention, but on the other side of that equation, you're faced with the difficult task of initiating the reformation of those critical areas: perceptions, values, goals, and relationships. You enter into a pivotal stage I refer to as *indecisive slumber*. This stage is usually the initial reaction of the fall season. It is that reluctant mind-set drawing from the last-ditch effort of comfort-zone conditioning to preserve what was and always have been. It is what you feel before crossing the threshold of complacency and landing into personal growth and transformation. The first step across this threshold is always a struggle, but crossing this threshold of complacency is a must.

Chapter 7 will highlight some major aspects to the decisions you'll have to make. Be confidently poised and decide to cross over the threshold of complacency into the realm of proactive decision making. Here are a few suggestions that I think will assist you in overcoming indecision. Firstly, you must be aware of the reason you need to change. Nothing in the past has brought you the joys and successes you've so deeply desired up to this point. You must settle in your spirit that you're determined to become your best self. It is not about becoming better than anyone else; it is about you evolving into the person of destiny you were predetermined to be.

Secondly, prepare yourself mentally and spiritually for the

"cost factor" involved in personal change and success. Counting the cost in life's endeavors is not only a theological position, it is philosophical as well as practical. God, our source, through His Son, Jesus, spoke these simple yet profound words, "From everyone who has been given much, much will be demanded; and from the one who has been entrusted with much, much more will be asked" (Luke 12:48). The cost will be discussed in more detail in the following chapter. But consider the fact that you must prepare yourself to pay the cost of severed associations, loss of friendships, rethinking your value systems, rejection, and many other factors depending on your specific situation. You may ask, is it all worth it? The answer is an overwhelming yes! Nothing in life is as important as personal development for the purpose of answering the call of destiny on your life, wherever it may lead.

Finally, stay focused on the goals and the results of the seasons of change. When you keep your eyes on the results and benefits, it will spark a renewed enthusiasm toward finishing what you've started. Let the truth be told, it is God who has begun this great work in you, and He will complete it. You've just come into the knowledge that much more exists for you in life than what you've experienced thus far. Something has brought you to this connecting point or, should I say, this crossroad of the plans and purposes of God concerning your life.

Once you discover who you are according to His plan, you will never be the same. Something extraordinary happens to an individual who peeks through the divine curtains of the heavenlies and for the first time in his or her life, gets a redemptive revelation—a clear view and direction about their future welfare. A divine light of hope is lit within that person, and it cannot be hidden. This experience cannot be ignored. Once tasted, nothing else can quench its thirst. Keep these growth principles before you, and change will seem as normal in your life as breathing air.

Epiphany
Preston Williams II

And suddenly my life comes full circle with intense meaning.
I'd stopped searching, feeling burnt out and universally
Out of place.

No vivid light at the end of a tunnel; no rainbow with a pot
Of gold at its base. Is this the Alpha of my present life or the
Omega of my past? Where, I wondered, am I on this mortal
Coil called life.

And suddenly, illumination; a manifestation of sorts, connected
My inner self as if the coil of life past engaged life present,
Causing a resurrection of life's future. Whether awake,
I cannot tell ... whether asleep, I cannot tell.
But this know ...

I discerned predestined unknowns, I witnessed not yet
Experienced victories; I harnessed unrealized
Potential. Purpose, deep within my then imprisoned
Mind, became exposed, released, and empowered ...
An epiphany

The preceding poem was written during a season of indecision. At one point, I had no idea what would become of me. And then, I realized I had to make some changes. I was already at the end of my rope, and nothing seemed to fit anymore. I had nothing left but a dream. I remember sharing those words with a complete stranger during our conversation on a flight from St. Croix, Virgin Islands. The gentleman, in his response to me, said, "You're in a very unique position." I asked him why he thought so, he replied, "A man with nothing, has nothing to lose ... take your dreams and run!" I now pass that same advice on to you as you enter into the arena of change. You have nothing to lose by making the needed adjustments in your life and following your heart toward your destiny. I close this chapter with a story that impacted my life in a powerful way. This story sums up the heart and soul behind my thrust for change, proper decisions, and the importance of fulfilling one's destiny. It is titled "A Tragedy."

An elderly man, in the final days of his life, is lying in bed alone. He awakens to see a large group of people clustered around his bed. Their faces are loving, but sad. Confused, the old man smiles weakly and whispers, "You must be my childhood friends … come to say good-bye. I am so grateful.

Moving closer, the tallest figure gently grasps the old man's hand and replies, "Yes, we are your best and oldest friends, but long ago you abandoned us; for we are the unfulfilled promises of your youth. We are the unrealized hopes, dreams, and plans that you once felt deeply in your heart but never pursued. We are the unique talents that you never refined, the special gifts you never discovered. Old friend, we have not come to comfort you, but to die with you."

Please don't let this be your experience. Will you leave footprints in the sands of time? How will your life be defined by others? How will your epitaph be read? Make the necessary changes and follow your dreams.

7

Determine Which Branches in Life to Trim Up, Cut Off, or Root Up

A man can only rise, conquer, and achieve by
lifting up his thoughts ...
By the right choice and true application of thought,
man ascends to the
Divine Perfection; by the abuse and wrong application of thought,
He descends below the level of the beast.

—James Allen[6]

Knowledge, understanding, and wisdom: these are the components of mind renewal and personal transformation in life. Knowledge is the acquisition of information. Understanding is the ability to correctly interpret the knowledge acquired with a sense of clarity. And wisdom, it is the ability to properly apply knowledge and understanding to life's diverse circumstances, maximizing the potential of the results. You will find these three components critical as you proceed toward determining which modifications are necessary for your personal growth. The knowledge and understanding gained in the process of your seasonal experiences are of utmost importance. We are to utilize these nuggets of illumination gained along with the precision of wisdom.

According to James Allen, by the right choices and proper

application of thought, or in this case illuminated thought, you open yourself to God's kingdom—the realm of the Divine Perfection. It is He who, in turn, mends the connecting dots of maturity, releasing or triggering the things that belong to your peace: provisions, protection, and potential. You experience the benefit of growing toward maturity by your right choices, conceived in the sphere of change.

The words of King Solomon in the book of Ecclesiastes best exemplify these three components: knowledge, understanding, and wisdom. He expands our dimension of thought and integrates the experiences of life in the realm of seasonal changes. According to Solomon, each experience is divinely time-calibrated for a specific purpose. In his poetic book, the king gives us the key to understanding life's many experiences. He says, "To everything, there is a season and a time to every purpose" (Ecclesiastes 3:1). This verse of Scripture was the seal of confirmation I needed for writing this book. As I continued to read the wisdom God imparted to Solomon, I noticed a relative but nonexhaustive list of timed events and circumstances in life that would do all of us well to embrace. For the purpose of developing this chapter, I particularly focused on the event, "A time to embrace, and a time to refrain from embracing."

I elected to use this particular event to parallel the fall season of life. Some view this as a separate, distinct event. Although this may be true to some degree, I believe this to be a group of events happening simultaneously as an exchange, or modification, of one's present experience for personal growth. A new level in life demands rearrangement of one's thought-life as well as how one acts out one's life. In reference to my particular focus, I submit that this is representative of the time to embrace the relationships, perceptions, and possessions that are potentially healthy to your personal development. With proper guidance and relational maintenance (pruning), they will prove to be a positive influence in your life.

On the flip side of this fall season parallel, lies the challenge.

It is the time in the perfecting process to release. This is a time to refrain from embracing the relationships, perceptions, and possessions that are potentially unhealthy and hazardous to your personal development. These are those people or things that conflict with your new lease on life. They represent individuals who choose not to support your new goals. They are those whose agenda was constructed to keep you in the same sphere of experiences year after year. Their acceptance of you was conditional, that is, only if you settled for nothing more than your existing state in life. Pitiful, isn't it? Unfortunately, this happens more in life than you know.

Wisdom is the ability to properly apply knowledge and understanding to life's diverse circumstances, maximizing the potential of the results

The pruning and rooting up process begins at this point. A skillful landscaper knows what parts of a tree can be salvaged and what parts should be completely detached. Who knows the nature of your life and all the details of your present situation better than God? He is the skillful landscaper, and you are the laborer. Together, you and God will initiate the pruning and rooting up process. This was discussed in chapter 5. This process takes place after personal inspection and after you've resolved in yourself that you will allow Him to empower you to make the necessary changes needed for your personal growth. It is He who will impress upon your heart which branches of your life are suitable for salvaging and those that are dead weight and require full detachment.

Through the pitfalls in my own life, I learned from experience. So by the time I entered into the fall season of my life, I was keenly aware of the people, perceptions, and possessions that would be affected by the modifying process. I was also aware of those that required complete detachment or separation. The challenge I grapple with is whether we will allow the process that requires thorough pruning and trimming to be completed. If we do, the priceless reward will be ours, my friend!

In this chapter, I explore some ways to help you determine which category to assign to each challenging area of your life. Determining which branches to trim up and which ones to cut off parallels you to a tree during the maintenance process. On the surface, the determining factors are simple. If a branch was affected during the infestation period but not totally damaged, then the solution is to *trim up* that branch and salvage the portion that has life in it, as this can restore life to the whole tree. On the other hand, if the branch is so infected that it rots, it means that it no longer has life, neither can it give life to the tree; the solution would be to completely *sever* that branch from the tree, so preservation and future growth will be allowed. Finally, if a tree is showing no life and bearing no fruit, it is unprofitable to its environment. That entire tree must be *rooted up*.

My personal journey through life, along with experiences individuals have shared with me during counseling sessions, have led me to conclude that these three principles are necessary for self-preservation and personal growth. No one is exempt from the transitions in life that mandate the use of at least one of these principles. At the very least, you will uncover the fragility and the strength of each relationship. So let's briefly examine these three simple maintenance principles.

Principle 1—Trimming Up

Life, like a tree, is made up of many parts, all of which are needed for the total structure of the tree. The major parts of a tree are its roots, trunk, branches, leaves, flowers, and seeds. These components are vital to the tree's growth, development, and reproduction. Phase one in the maintenance process is trimming up. The trimming up of the tree maintains the form of the tree; removes weak, sickly, or unproductive branches; and rejuvenates old or unhealthy plants. In life, this process is equally important in terms of determining which people, perceptions, and/or possessions to trim up. You must identify which, if not all, of these are distorting your life form. If you've embraced what you've read thus far, you should have decided to pursue life differently. If so, you are, in effect, changing form.

Your mind is being renewed with fresh insights, new perceptions; hence, you are being transformed into the new person of destiny. To this day, it amazes me how family, friends, and colleagues will view you once they witness a change in your life's focus. There are those who will affirm the new you, some will hold you suspect, and others will flatly despise you. Something happens internally and externally to an individual who has received positive, life-changing nurture. They seem taller, more confident, independent, and in control (the power to subdue and exercise dominion) of their circumstances.

Almost immediately, you will notice a shift in the way people respond to you and the way you respond to people. You will become more alert in your surroundings, and there will be a keener sensitivity to how your relationships are impacting you. As a result, your renewed perception will discern those branches in your life that are weak and sickly. These are the individuals who will drain your enthusiasm, and because of their limited perceptions, they tend to weaken your confidence and dim your vision of the future. You've arranged your existence around them. They are not forces or individuals outside of your realm of relationships. These are individuals that directly influence you. You've come to depend on them as a source of comfort and relativity.

Heretofore, they've made you feel like you're a part and that you belong to something special. But somehow, you know something is wrong, because the relationship(s) has caused your life to stagnate. Here is a special note: *The limited results of your life are in direct proportion to their limited knowledge and understanding about your life situation.* The fact that you've exalted these individuals to the ranks of credible authority in your life causes them to have preeminent influence in and over you. In other words, your success and happiness in life is dependent on how they view you and how they expect you to live out your life. Their perceptions, personal philosophy, and goals in life become your own; as a result, you take on the form of those who influence you.

As dismal as this may sound, it happens all too often. To live in the shadow of others, never finding your own unique voice and place in life is tragic. There is no wonder King Solomon advises that there is a time to embrace and a time to refrain from embracing. The determining factor in the trimming-up process is to identify who will embrace the new form that you've chosen to accept for your life: the new you. Obviously, people help to shape our perceptions concerning how we live and what we infer as truth. To change your perception, you must first change your position concerning the influences in your life. It is important to allow God to be your primary influence. In conforming, we must use His image as a pattern in order for it to be effectual. After all, we are to be an extension of His uniqueness in the world. In Him, we discover our true form. In God, we will find an inexhaustible strength, a voice that will impact our generation, and a purposefully orchestrated place in this world within which we're to flourish.

Dr. I. V. Hilliard of Houston, Texas, said something to me at a leadership conference that tremendously impacted my life. He said, "When my heart is right toward God, He obligates himself to orchestrate my life, to bring me into the knowledge of the things I need to know, and also into the company of people I need to know that are critical for my success and destiny in life." I have never forgotten this powerful truth. It is within the context of Dr. Hilliard's statement that I have gained this truth: God has chosen certain people and experiences to impart His ways and means *for* our lives, as well as *in* our lives, for our success and destiny. At this point, you may ask, So how do I proceed with the process of reevaluating those who are presently in my life? Here are a few questions to consider as you begin the sorting-out process.

- Which people in my life can flow with me in my new form of life?
- Although they may not understand the new me, can they adjust?
- Will they accept me as an independent thinking person?
- Am I positively nurtured through this relationship, or am I being spoon-fed unhealthy perceptions and ideas?
- Is our friendship dependent on my agreeing and following their lead?
- Do we have the kind of relationship where we have the right to agree to disagree when there is conflict due to a personal conviction?

These are just a few of the important questions you should ponder as you move toward the trimming-up process. If it is possible to maintain a nurturing relationship amid the adjustments and the changes in your life, as well as in the life of the other individual, then trimming up is the course of action to take. There are wonderful relationships that thrive on the personal development and upward mobility of the other party. They are not threatened by each other's progress; in fact, they encourage each other to pursue the best in life, and when one achieves a new level in life or gets that long-awaited promotion, they genuinely celebrate the achievement together. This celebration of success is possible because in no small way, their relationship, if it has been a flexible, nurturing one, has contributed to the strength of that person's life. I believe the Bible identifies this as "edifying one another" (Romans 14:19).

Trimming up, unlike cutting off, does not require severing

relationships. Because the relationships have some level of benefit in your life, this process only requires that you trim their level of authority in your life. In essence, maintain your camaraderie with your acquaintances, allow room for personal growth in their lives as well, but set new boundaries—lessen their influence in your decision-making process. After all, as the old adage says, "If the blind man leads a blind man, both will fall into a pit" (Matthew 15:14*b* NIV). Examine the terrain of your friendships—collaboration, cooperation, and competition. Then rethink appropriate limitations. If these three terrains of relationships have the appropriate limitations, everyone involved possesses the potential for growth. Undergirding this potential for growth is a fundamental trust that the other has your best interests at heart.

To change your perception you must first change your position concerning the influences in your life

Likewise, perceptions, if they are not conducive to your new form in life, must be trimmed up or readjusted to fit the new you. By now, it is no secret that we function and respond to life based on perceptions. Those perceptions are influenced by people we've embraced as authoritative figures in our lives, whether through conversations, media, or experiences. These authoritative figures, for the most part, have developed our views concerning life. Our major challenge now, after the "people issue," is choosing to operate in a different frame of mind. It is choosing to respond to life differently and to replace old concepts with new ones as a result of your new direction in life. We are transformed as individuals only after we've elected to change our perceptions, ideals, and former truths. We renew our minds with that which is truly nurturing and profitable (Roman 12:2*a*). The trimming-up process seeks to salvage potentially nurturing relationships. Hopefully, in the process, the other party will also grow as an individual and be inspired to seek truth for their own life. For the most part, the relationship becomes a sharpening tool in each person's life.

A final aspect of the trimming-up process relates to the benefit of continuing this pruning process even in the "fruitage" season (see part 4: "The Spring Season") of life. If this process is performed during a period of vigorous growth, it could also result in the increase of new flowers. In humanity, that equates to prosperity and personal well-being. Another important feature in the trimming-up process is that cuts are made just above the buds that point in the direction toward which the branches are desired to grow. Likewise, you should trim relationships in the direction of your purpose in life.

Make sure that the branches you've chosen to remain on the tree are nurtured toward the direction of your goals in life. Understand that in life you have dream sharers, and dream destroyers. Determine which of the two you are dealing with, and begin the pruning process. The question is asked, "How can two walk together unless they agree?" (Amos 3:3). This passage encourages relationships whose foundations are built on shared values, precepts, and principles that govern our unique lives. Some individuals who are a part of your life have issues that could hinder you and your relationship with them but are willing to make some needed changes to improve themselves. These changes will improve their relationship with you as you embrace the changes relative to the new you.

Principle 2—Cutting Off

As we move forward to the next level of the pruning process, which is the cutting off, you will notice that the adjustment in the relationship requires a detachment of the larger branch. It definitely requires the cutting off of the entire unhealthy relationship. In this type of situation, trimming up is not sufficient. I must reiterate: it is important to note that each branch represents individual relationships in your life. The extended small branches and leaves are the fruit of the branches—individual relationships. To salvage the branches (individual relationships), it is necessary to trim up the small branches and leaves that have signs of decay (issues that jeopardize proper nurturing).

The cutting-off process of pruning is the more difficult of the two processes (trimming up and cutting off). Because these larger branches are individuals we've come to know, love, and trust, we've allowed ourselves to get emotionally bonded. Part of the other person's heart and soul reaches out to connect with you, and part of your heart and soul reaches out to connect with that person. Your heart and soul become webbed—woven into each other. This can be good if you're bonding with the right individuals, those who will help you live out your dreams and those who endorse your change for a better life.

But it can be lethal if you're bonding with individuals who are not nurturers, those who smother your dreams, steering you to a life that is less than significant and, at times, pointless and lacking purpose. I've found that even though these individuals belittle our individuality, downgrade our sexuality, blight our hopes, and cripple our aspirations, detachment from them can be quite traumatic because of the emotional bonding developed over a period of time. This dilemma causes me to pause as I vividly remember such moments in my life. So, as a voice of reason in your life, I caution you to be careful of the webs you weave between yourself and others. The emotional trauma during this stage of pruning can sometimes be unbearable, the physical effects draining, the spiritual impact immobilizing, and the social cost could result in self-inflicted isolation and low self-esteem. Disheartening as it may be, detachment is often a must for your growth and future well-being.

As I researched the topic of pruning, I had the opportunity to speak with an experienced landscaper concerning an additional concept I came across. The concept, at first, did not seem very important to me. That changed, however, as I discussed it with the professional landscaper. He expanded my knowledge and understanding of its value.

The concept contends that when large branches are removed from any tree, the cut should be made close to the trunk and then covered for a time. The value of this procedure is to ensure that no residual growth occurs. In relationships, we are to sever all close impairing attachments, whether they are emotional, financial, or philosophical. And as the tree cut is covered so as not to give it any source for life, we, too, must cover our severed areas with truth so that nurturing of negative influences will not be provided by its life source. These are: doubt, wrong thought, desperation, loneliness, and hopelessness. In other words, don't allow any attachments that are not nurturing into your new life. They will only cause resuscitation to the life out of and above which you've chosen to transcend.

Principle 3—Rooting Up

We have come to the final process. From time to time, this process will be essential to the life of the tree. This process in life is usually the most overlooked. It is referred to as rooting up. After the process of trimming up and cutting off, you may have to check the soil where you're rooted. If after you've taken all of the preliminary precautions to maintain your life properly you find yourself still experiencing a sense of hopelessness, a lack of enthusiasm toward achieving your goals, and the frustration of a "treadmill" mentality, this could be sign of a deeper problem. To save a plant, many times the plant must be repotted, and to save a tree, it might become necessary to uproot it. The course of action sometimes necessary to preserve the life of the tree or the plant is to reposition it entirely. Make no mistake, this process is one that requires proper evaluation, relocation planning, and knowledge of the process. All of this will be discussed in chapter 8.

Trees are held in place by anchoring organs called roots. In addition to anchoring the tree, roots also absorb water and minerals from the soil through tiny structures called root hairs. The root system is the vehicle through which nutrients in the form of water and minerals are carried from the soil upward through the wood cells to the leaves. If the soil is compromised and unhealthy, the tree will suffer the same effects as if no trimming up or cutting off of the branches occurred. Soon, decaying/rotting will take place.

In life, this translates to the fact that we must consider or rethink our work environment, place of leisure, place of abode, and yes, even our place of worship. We must all take a closer look at where we've chosen to plant our feet in life. These places represent the soil in which we're planted. It is where we anticipate the nutrients for life. The question we must ask ourselves is: Are the places we've chosen for our source of income, resort, residence, and worship spiritual nurturing or fertile ground? If the answer is no, rooting up is the proper course of action to take. This should be approached in a spirit of patience and guidance. There is a very small margin of error in this particular area of pruning. Therefore, it is imperative that we take caution. Wait on God, that innate voice, to speak. Wait for Him to orchestrate our move. It is He who will assist us in finding our "fertile crescent" in life.

When you find yourself feeling anxious about your situation and you don't know what to do, ponder this Scripture passage, "He performeth the thing that is appointed for me... The Lord will perfect that which concerneth me" (Job 23:14).

8
Detaching: Initiating the Pruning Process

A wrong decision isn't forever; it can always be reversed. The losses from delayed decisions are forever; they can never be retrieved.

—J. K. Galbraith

As we conclude part 2, the fall season, one can't help but wonder where do I go from here? This next step is most pivotal and very crucial. It involves initiating everything we know to be true about our present situation. If we've listened close enough to the voice of truth, our awareness should be overflowing with fresh illumination concerning life, accompanied with a "things to do" list. The process of detaching or pruning, whether it is a partial trimming or complete detachment, requires a certain mental attitude. This is true anytime action is summoned to a particular situation in life; the proper mental attitude is proportionately essential in fulfilling the call of truth's resolve.

This attitude is courage. In chapter 6, we found that the process of dealing with indecision about coming to terms with the changes requires courage. It will be even more essential now that you must to take action and initiate the changes that you know are necessary. The opposite of courage is fear. It causes retardation, destructive inhibition, and many other negatives. Avoid redundancy! I encourage you to reread the portion in chapter 6 that deals with "The Spirit of Fear and Its Fruit." One element I must impart to you in this chapter is the dimension of *innate freedom* and *spiritual rebirth*. This materializes when we walk and respond to life in the attitude of courage. I urge you to consider this statement: "Courage keeps us moving forward even when we don't totally understand why." Think of this phrase, speak it, and internalize it, "trembling but trusting." There are times we will move forward and act with a sense of ease and confidence, but there are times when we will have to move forward even if the sense of ease and confidence is not there. This is what I mean by "trembling but trusting." It is a trust that transcends our understanding, allowing us to experience certain victories and successes in life. We must take this kind of trust with a step-by-step approach in dealing with the challenges in life until the freedom of this rebirth becomes a natural expectancy in our lives, irrespective of the circumstances that surround us.

Baltasar Gracian, a Spanish philosopher (1601–58), gave a sound charge to those who choose to be initiators of courage. He said, "So be reborn in courage, in intellect, in happiness, and in all else. Dare to renew your brilliance, dawning many times, like the sun, only changing your surrounding." I believe the essence of Baltasar's charge was to challenge us to think and act outside of the glass house mentality. He calls forth a new being, one who no longer functions in the shallow waters of inferiority but in the newness of courage, intellect, happiness, and all that applies to the new *you* of destiny's making. This is representative of operating in a sense of personal ownership of your life and the choices you make in it. Personal ownership comes with the burden of responsibility. The Bible says, "To whom much is given, much will be required" (Luke 12:48). This is certainly a prime example of the thrust of the philosopher's charge to keep.

There is no gift given to you that is more valuable than life. It is, therefore, your God-given responsibility to be a good steward of it. All of our experiences are our own to sort out and know which ones to maintain with a sense of divine accountability.

When you embrace this truth, you must realize that it would be detrimental if you allow such a valuable asset of creation to be improperly tarnished by bad influence. It is your responsibility to carefully guard your life; take dominion over your circumstances, constantly prune the critical areas for maximum personal growth and effective relational development. If not, you will become victims of life's circumstances. Life will live you instead of you living life! William Hines, in his book *Leaving Yesterday Behind*, expressed the importance of taking ownership of personal life and choices. Following are two excerpts from his book:

1. I have bought several used cars in my life. I realized the risk involved in buying a second-hand car. The previous owner may not have taken care of it. He may not be telling me all the problems with it. But once I buy it, it is mine for better or for worse. The car is my responsibility now.

2. Taking ownership of ourselves is important. I may not be responsible for what happened to me growing up, but I am responsible for what I do now. It might be much easier on the ego to blame others for our problems. If we can shift the blame, then we become victims and as a victim it is much easier to garner sympathy for our plight. But people who remain victims never fully mature. [7]

Hines's statement upholds pruning as a prerequisite to growth and maturity. Once you begin to prune, you will notice a refreshing sense of personal independence. There will be a release from imposed obligations that did not represent your convictions. As was stated earlier, you will not shift blame to others; instead, you will take ownership. You will admit to what you've allowed others to impose on you in the past and use it as the fuel you need to make the necessary changes. No longer will you be a puppet at the end of the string of manipulation. You will now be the courageous initiator of your purpose and fulfiller of your destiny enabled by the "I am" of Israel's exodus, the divine source of life. Historically, the nation of Israel, enabled by God, had to initiate detachment from the source of their enslavement in order to gain that which was predetermined for them to possess. You know the story. They were led by God, who manifested himself in a pillar of cloud by day and a pillar of fire by night. Yes, they were led by the One who cannot lie, and it was that light of truth that lit their pathway toward freedom and prosperity. As you walk in the brilliant light of the truth of your newfound life, it is important to remember the three specific areas that will be affected by the detaching process. They are: people, perception, and place (see "Rooting Up," chapter 7). Prepare now to deal with these sensitive areas.

Now that you're walking in the dimension of light, detachment in many areas will be automatic. Just think of the natural light of day consuming the darkness of night. This is a simple message of truth that nature teaches us. The light of truth will expose the darkness in the heart of any misguided individual involved in your life. When this occurs, one of two things will happen. The misguided individual will either be corrected by the light of truth, remain in your life, and grow with you, which is trimming up—or reject the light of truth in your life and separate, that is, a complete severing, cutting off/falling away.

Detaching People (Modifying Relationships)

Let me inform you that I have no intention of giving explicit directions as to how you should initiate the detaching process. The detachment of individuals is based on many variables. These variables involve unique and diverse elements of the relationships that exist. Additionally, you are more aware of the distinguishing temperaments of those with whom you're involved. I will give only one absolute as it relates to detaching; that absolute is *love*.

Love should be the basis of all correction, reproof, and rebuke. This is true even to you, as the initiator, as well as the individual subject to the detaching process.

The following adage and scriptural wisdom should be the rule of thumb in this process, "Do unto others as you would have them do unto you." Simply stated, it is most effective, and morally proper, to respond to others in the manner you would desire to be responded to if you were in a similar situation. Make no mistake about it, just as you are in a season that requires pruning others, so are others in similar season, and you may be the object of their pruning. So, approach the pruning process with empathy because you, too, are a friend of someone who may very well be in the valley of decision about how to approach you in their pruning process.

The key in all of this is not to take the change too personally; be open, no matter which end of the relationship you find yourself. The pruning process is about personal well-being and growth. So, keep in mind the reason you're pruning and the attitude of love, as it is the primary prerequisite in initiating what needs to be done. As you are modifying your life for personal success, fulfillment, and well-being, understand that the detaching process exposes the individual involved to the opportunity of viewing your love from an unpopular perspective. This unpopular view will expose the flip side of any true friendship: tough love and honesty. This comes in the form of loving and respecting an individual enough to give them the opportunity to embrace life in the spirit of change with you or to find other breeding grounds that are more conducive to their comfort zones (way of life).

The beauty in true friendship is that you have the right to choose the degree of association and influence you will permit others to have in your life. Relationships become emotionally taxing when this line is crossed. The imposing of one's values on another is in total contrast to friendly advice and solicited opinion. The imposing friend expects you to do exactly what he says. If you oppose, you're labeled as one who doesn't take counsel well. This generally leads to slow-building tension between the two, resulting in either a harsh dissolution of the relationship or the advisee yielding to the control of the adviser. In the case of friendly advice and solicited opinion, you're given nuggets of advice wherein you have the right to determine what is best for you. A mature, advising individual does not expect a verbatim application of counsel, nor does he fume if you decide that his advice, though good, is not what is best for you at that time.

The latter is the ideal relationship. It functions with a healthy respect for a person's right to choose what is suitable to his or her unique circumstances in life. The former is an unhealthy relationship; temporary separation or permanent detachment is necessary. Separation, in many ways, brings pause into the life of both individuals involved. It is a time of corrective reflection and introspection. Use this time to look closely at your life as a whole. Set some standards concerning your associations in terms of moving forward. With a skillful approach, begin trimming up and cutting off in the crucial areas. With your heart and mind fixed on where you're growing in the realm of destiny and purpose, proceed with courage and in the spirit love. Here are a few things to be mindful of and to avoid.

- Be careful of the temptation to reattach to unhealthy relationships. It is a strong temptation that must be avoided.
- Avoid the temptation to fill the void left by the detaching process with someone who is just as unhealthy and functions in the same mind-set as the previous person. My personal experience has validated that only a spiritual relationship can fill innate voids. God is the beginning of true fulfillment. Everything else should be tempered by that relationship.
- Be careful of your new associations. Make sure they share your desire for personal growth and spiritual well-being. Note: *Association breeds assimilation;*

assimilation, if it is not nurturing, places you right back into emotional, financial, relational, and spiritual bondage from which you came, distorting the reality of the growth that you experienced.

- Avoid pessimists, "the glass is half empty" individuals, and embrace optimists, the dream-sharing ones enthusiastic about life's possibilities.
- Avoid the spirit of pride. We aren't searching to become better than anyone else; our objective is to become our best selves and to surround ourselves with those who are on the same quest in life.

These are just a few items of caution to assist you in your process of pruning and to keep you on track during your journey to "becoming." Your experiences will unfold many other pros and cons as you develop. Take note of them, and learn the principles that lie hidden in the experiences they bring to your life.

Modifying Perceptions (Mind Renewal and Thought-Conditioning)

Perceptions, among other things, are better described as one's ultimate experience of the world. These experiences involve people, places, and philosophies. Everything we are is the sum total of all we've experienced from birth until the present. Our passionate embrace of these experiences, along with our resolve toward them, develop what we call our personal philosophy, good, bad, or indifferent. It is this philosophy of life that needs pruning. Like people, perceptions can either be modified or completely replaced. Personal transformation is dependent on mind renewal. Mind renewal is only possible when we decide to rethink our perceptions based solely on our personal philosophies.

In order to measure the validity of your perceptions, you must measure them by truth. Truth declares that you can identify a tree by the fruit it bears. If it bears no fruit, then it would be reasonable to say that this nurturing agent is insufficient. Likewise, if your life is not bearing its predestined fruit, the nurturing agent must be replaced. Your perceptions are the nurturing agents. They are what fuel your actions and temper your behavior.

Pruning your perceptions is similar to pruning relationships. The only difference is that, unlike relationships, your perceptions are continuous thoughts that govern your existence. They cannot be detached, but they can be modified. You cannot take time away from your thoughts, and you cannot demographically separate yourself from your mind. So, modifying your perceptions is your only recourse as a pruning tool. This is done through thought-conditioning. Eric Fellman, president and CEO of Peale Center, said, "The principle behind thought-conditioning is similar to that behind air-conditioning. Just as air-conditioning changes the atmosphere of a room, keeping it fresh and healthy, thought-conditioning changes the atmosphere of your mind, giving clarity, peak health, and vitality to your life." Take a moment and digest that principle.

The atmosphere of your mind requires pruning for fresh insight. Improper influences cloud your mental atmosphere, stifle the innate creativity, and cap the unlimited potential God has imparted to us all for abundant living. Fellman also said, "Thoughts are the basic ingredients of all phases of the inner life. They're the expression of the seeds of belief, kindness, and optimism; they're the building blocks of solid faith, hope, and love. Furthermore, they provide the energy conducive to be sent out by a pure spirit to shape and build our mental, emotional, and physical being. Without healthy powerful thoughts providing this energy, all efforts at self-control, discipline, and change will be ineffective."[8] From this, we can see that pruning your thoughts is the driving force behind modifying your perceptions toward life. Our behavior or response to life is the outward manifestation of our innate thoughts and perceptions. To change our behavior, we must modify our thoughts and refocus our perceptions.

Since perceptions are derived by exposure to external influences, we must consider the fact that if we're to change the atmosphere of our mind, we must begin to rethink our surroundings—the atmospheric condition of where we rest, resort, work, and worship. We must ask the inevitable question, am I receiving positive nurturing in these surroundings? As we flow into the final stage of the pruning process, rooting up, remember, you have a most precious gift given to mankind: the gift of personal choice. Every day, we make choices that will inevitably return to us with consequences to test our strength and character. Use it wisely.

Rooting-Up Places (Rethinking Demographics —Work, Resort, Worship)

The people and perception perspective of pruning leads us to the final and very important segment of the process, which is rooting up. Unlike people and perceptions, rooting up requires us to reevaluate our places of influence. Places of influence are just as impacting as the negative propaganda of the media or the controlling pessimism of some individuals. In most books that deal with personal empowerment, not much is said about home, "the hangout" (place of leisure and wind-down), work, and church. I consider these to be major places of influence and interaction for adults. Our self-worth, directly and indirectly, is shaped by the people in these environments.

The sociological perspective states that individuals are influenced and shaped by their environment. Have you ever spent time in different parts of your city, or even other cities, and noticed that each place has its own defining presence? The impression of that city's presence will immediately impact you in one of two ways: your senses will either begin to approve of and conform to the mood of the city, or to disapprove, resulting in your becoming uneasy with the experience innately.

Similar to the impact the presence and ambiance of any city has on us, the places we spend our time from day to day impact us positively or negatively as well. We either conform to or conflict with the defining presence of the environment. Environments play a huge part in how we view ourselves and the future outlook we have on life. It becomes our frame of reference for decision making in many cases. For example, I was told that in certain parts of Alaska, residents wear hats with light attachments because depression is prevalent due to the dreary environment. Also, it is said that in Seattle, Washington, the suicide rate is very high as compared to any other city in the United States. This is attributed to the excessive cloudiness and rain year round.

These areas are influenced by natural climate and weather conditions; people have no control over those effects. If you lived in one of those types of environmental conditions and you were affected negatively to the point of personal hurt and harm, then the rooting-up process for you would involve planning to relocate to a more agreeable city or state. Since I have been living in south Florida, each year I witness snowbirds relocate to this state for health reasons. This is significant to the rooting-up process. God has given even animals the instinct to apply this principle at the appropriate time and for the right reason.

If rooting up is a recommended solution for physical health, then it is equally important for you to root up as it relates to your personal well-being, psychologically as well as spiritually. Let me suggest that rooting up does not necessarily require drastic relocation. My advice is for you to rethink these places of influences and replace them with more nurturing environments where applicable. Unlike how you trimmed up and cut off interaction with persons previously discussed, rooting up is not dependent on others participating in the process. This is an individual endeavor. It is you removing yourself from places that have historically proven to be a negative influence in your life. The environments that I address in this closing chapter are not influenced by the natural climate or by weather conditions but by the dominant mind-set of the people inhabiting these places.

Unlike people and perceptions, rooting up requires us to reevaluate our places of influence

Of the four rooting-up places named previously, the home is the only one where you have control. You have exclusive rights to share your input as to how things should be modified to suit your personal, unique environmental needs. The others are more corporal in their makeup. Work and worship most likely already have an organizational structure that do not require nor solicit your input. A smorgasbord of free-for-all expressions would already exist in a cool-out, wind-down environment (leisure spots), which also does not require nor solicit your input. These four places are where society dictates that we receive our nurturing and moral acceptance. This is true in many respects, but we must reconstruct our thoughts and evaluate the places where we plant ourselves. These places affect our entire behavior pattern. This happens because we convince ourselves that these are where our true value is determined.

Performance in the places of work and worship, and the approval of others in the place of leisure, seem to be the motivating factors that drive us to plant our lives in certain environments. It is summed up with the overwhelming evidence of truth that we just want to be accepted, not for who we truly are, but for the "whom" and the "what" it takes to be a member of the groups that occupy the places we frequent. According to Robert S. McGee, "If we base our worth on our abilities or the fickle approval of others, then our behavior will reflect the insecurity, fear, and anger that come from such instability."[9]

In the home, we must rethink our operation and develop an openness or discussion in order to create the proper ambiance for personal growth. At the workplace, there is very little you can do to change policies that are conducive to your personal needs. This depends on the values of the company you work for, the people you fraternize with, and the conflict of whether or not you are fulfilled in what you chose to do for your livelihood. In the place of worship, again you're in an environment that operates by predetermined denominational, institutional dictates or the personalized decrees of boards and internal influential cliques. We must be honest with ourselves and determine whether we're being properly nurtured spiritually in such environments. It is our duty to question whether we are growing spiritually. If you find that these three areas do not provide challenge, nurturance, or personal fulfillment, then rooting up is the proper course of action to take.

Important Note: *Let me make it crystal clear, I am not advocating that being a part a religious institution or organization is not nurturing. On the contrary, I endorse ecclesiastical accountability. My position is based on truth versus ideologies that are not balanced. Those ideologies that find their way into places of worship prove to be more harmful than nurturing. Ideology constantly changes; it is from man. Truth is immutable; it is from God. So, if the church is to be a nurturer and supporter of the truth, ideology and truth can never be mixed.*

As it is with gardening, not all soils have enough nutrients or the right balance of nutrients to care for the plant. Plants remove nutrients from the soil as they grow, so these nutrients must be replaced for the soil to remain productive. Likewise, we draw nutrients from our environments, but once the soil of these places proves to be no longer productive and nurturing, one of two resolves must be initiated. Like the gardener, (1) we either enhance the soil by adding fertilizer (that which breeds life), a material that contains one or more of the nutrients plants need, or (2) the plant is rooted up and moved to a more nurturing, productive soil.

For personal application, with patience, research, and wisdom, fertilize and till the soil at home for revitalization and productivity. At work, play, and worship, think about your needs and prepare yourself for repositioning and finding life's proper soil for replanting. I conclude this chapter by reiterating the thought-provoking words of Baltasar Gracian, "Dare to renew your brilliance, dawning many times, like the sun, only changing your surrounding."

PART III
Winter: The Season of Introspection

When to the sessions of sweet silent thought
I summon up remembrance of things past,
I sigh the lack of many a thing I sought,
And with old woes new wail my dear times' waste

—William Shakespeare

9

The Cold Serenity of Winter: The Season of Meditation and Personal Reflection

*It is next to impossible to find a quiet place for
meditation these days. If you do not carry a calm
spot in your soul, it will not help much to find
one on the outside*

—Vance Havner

The winter, a season of meditation, a time of inner examination of one's life away from outside censorship. It has been said that the number-one shortcoming of man at the close of each century is that, "We lead unexamined lives. Most men have not carefully chiseled their lives view by a personal search for truth and obedience to God."[10] Instead, we rush from task to task, busy! We don't call enough time-outs to reflect on life's larger meaning and purpose. Rather, we live myopically from day to day; we live under the tyranny of today's problems.

Meditation often involves turning attention to a single point of reference. In this book, the single point of reference is you—the focus of inner examination—self-regulation of attention in the service of self-inquiry. We look into our innermost being to see what we've ignored, to test our present standards, and to be illumined by truth, a revelation of that special purpose God has for our lives. The purpose He reveals might be somewhat different than the one you are pursuing at present. Meditation connects and confirms that special purpose in your life. But it is not without a cost.

When I was in my early thirties, I made a decision that would impact my life forever. The decision would prove to challenge my vocational associations, personal relationships, and family. Little did I know just how much my life would change, and how cruel those who once attached the label "friend" to our association could be. Because of my personal convictions, it became necessary to sever ties with an organization that I love and cherish to this day.

The foundation this organization laid for me in my youth has been an invaluable asset to my adulthood. Anyway, I came to a point in my life that required rethinking specific concerns, passions, and inner conflicting principles. My life was changing, and God was orchestrating its rhythm. I remember years earlier, my father saying to me as a young man that I would have to make some decisions in life that neither my mother nor he would understand. He further said that I would have to choose either to do what was popular and continue on the common path, or decide to follow what I knew in my heart to be true. I was just completing high school then. I'm sure that when my father spoke those words of wisdom, it was meant for the young me dealing with the tough choices common to anyone transitioning from high school to college.

Well, needless to say, this bit of advice followed me to a place in my life that neither of us could have fathomed. I followed my heart at the cost of friendships, associations, and social acceptance. I didn't know it then, but I know it now … I was entering the winter season of my life. It was a season that I not only had to go through but also had to endure with patient hope. Initially, it was disorienting. It was as if one day I was on top of the world and on my way toward the common paths of organizational succession. Then, with one courageously initiated, heartfelt decision … I found myself alone.

Meditation often involves turning attention to a single point of reference

I was ostracized and scorned by peers and misunderstood by some family members. I was avoided by acquaintances. I must admit, at times I questioned whether I had done the right thing. I must pause here for a moment to say that, honestly, when your world is turned upside down, you *will* experience some degree of doubt. Don't let it consume you. Historically speaking, even Jesus, the Christ, had a moment of question. Do you remember? It is written that as Christ approached His final moment of purpose, He was overwhelmed by the pressures of His call to destiny and prayed, "If it be possible, let this cup pass from me." Was He overwhelmed by the moment? Yes. Did He give in to the temptation to abort His purpose? No. His statement of resolution was, "Nevertheless, thy will be done." I had always enjoyed the support of those who shared the same organizational affiliation, those who equally embraced the dream of becoming vessels of change and, with honor, submit to the rite of passage toward being the torch carriers of our generation. But, they were no more. I was labeled a defector, and I knew my life would never be the same.

Innately, the void created by my decision to initiate change in my life expanded with the dawning of each new day. The frustration of not being understood began to eat away at my innermost being. I became depressed and isolated. But, something wonderful happened to me during that time of isolation. I found the most valuable treasure anyone could ever find. I found that calm spot in my soul that connects the dots of a fragmented life and places everything into proper perspective. I realized that the winter season of my life would prove to be a double-edged sword. This season would prove to be a time of distancing myself from certain associations and relationships, but it would also be a time of self-discovery and development in the presence of God, the divine One. He would have me right where He's always wanted me … for himself. This would be a time of purposeful shaping without the distraction of outside influences. The winter of my life was upon me, and God was beckoning for my undivided attention.

So what is the winter season of life? What does it represent in life, and how does it parallel with nature's winter? The winter season of the year occurs between the fall and spring seasons each year. Relative to the focus of our discussion, it immediately follows the pruning season and precedes the budding season of personal growth and prosperity. Think about that for a moment: you're one season away from your next level, prosperity. I embrace the biblical and philosophical principle that teaches, "Once we begin to walk the path of truth and sojourn the road of destiny, we draw into our lives those things that belong to us in life to fulfill our purpose: provisions, protection, and prosperity." Personal initiative and taking ownership of your life have allowed you to successfully transition through the fall season.

If the transition was successful, you have a new sense of personal freedom, though, at the same time, you may be experiencing a reclusive time in your life. Family, friends, and associates are now aware of the new you that has emerged, along with the changes that accompanied this innate metamorphosis. Metaphorically speaking, you may be relationally experiencing what nature climatically gives off during the winter season—cold to freezing temperatures. In relationships, this describes the attitudes leveled toward you for having the audacity to change.

In many regions, winter is characterized by freezing temperatures. The fall/autumn gardening season has ended; the leaves have fallen, the limbs and branches have been trimmed up or cut off completely, and the endangered plants have been rooted up and prepped for safer environments until proper growth locations are found. Likewise, you have gone through a similar pruning process, and now you are experiencing the cold to frigid attitudes from those with whom some of these changes are directly involved. They are freezing you out from groups and places. These places that once served as pseudo-safe, nurturing environments have proven to be the nemesis of personal growth.

What was intended for hurt and harm will really prove beneficial in your winter season of shaping. Your winter season will make you withdraw into a quiet, personal place of introspection. This is a place that few individuals enter, and even fewer individuals desire. It is a place of pondering and meditation. Usually, life has us so busy we fail to take time out to ponder the vital aspects. Unfortunately, meditation is shunned as if it were a neo-voodoo practice. I say that with a smile on my face, because this was an actual response given to me during a conversation with a client in a counseling session. We were discussing the importance of "being still" and "meditating in the presence of God."

Much has been said about meditation today, but it is certainly nothing new. In biblical times, for example, we see where it was common practice of King David of Israel. He gave an essential paradigm for personal growth in the following paraphrased statements:

> Blessed is the man that walks not in the counsel of the ungodly, nor sits in the seat of the scornful, nor stands in the way of the sinner. But his delight is in the law of the Lord and on this law does he MEDITATE day and night; he shall be as a tree planted by rivers of water which bears its fruit in its season; its leaves also shall not whither, but whatsoever he does shall prosper. (Psalm 1:1–3)

Meditation is a deep, personal engagement in contemplation, especially of a spiritual or devotional nature. Its purpose is to gain proper perspective, wisdom, and progressive states of emotional well-being. Meditating helps us to control our life situations. It prevents the triggering of our false beliefs and the perceptions of our old human nature. With the negative influences distanced in your life, one way or another, you have the time in your winter season to be alone in your thoughts and with God. Although the "people" and "perception" aspect has been dealt with in previous chapters, there remains the element of continued maintenance of your thought-life. This element is the jewel of meditation. When we maintain our thought-life, this allows us to disassemble the debilitating issues and false beliefs of life and replace them with truth. Meditation is the key to maximizing the clarity and creative potential of our thought-life. It connects us to the Creator of all creations.

Like the seasons during your previous life, you can attempt to go through the winter transformation by depending only on your own abilities and natural mind, or you can, through meditation, seek God's guidance. I have always found it amazing and sometimes appalling how easy it is for many of us to turn to God as a last resort or an option during a crisis. As soon as He opens the door to resolving the crisis, in our limited and debilitating ways, we try to assume independent control of our lives as if we no longer need God's participation. This naïveté will almost always lead to reentry into the same or worse situations. Once you find yourself drowning in the consequences of having ignored God, that will trigger bouts of depression. It leaves you questioning outcomes, losing sleep, and dreading tomorrow, because you know the conflicting challenges you must contend with apart from your source.

The common denominator that links mankind and crosses all cultural, social, and financial boundaries is our need for a source higher than ourselves. It doesn't matter what station in life you are called to, from the president of the United States to the pastor of a small congregation, from the CEO of a major corporation to the janitor of that company. If God's participating presence, illuminating insight, and power corrected an area of your life that resulted in personal growth and prosperity, then you can be sure he is the continued *source* of your personal healing and progression. No status in life exempts you from this reality. The winter season in your life is about you, your thoughts, and God.

When we enter into this meditative season, our objective should be to rethink our position, our motives, and our future plans in life as they relate to His divine purpose.

Your winter season will make you withdraw into a quiet, personal place of introspection

The remainder of this chapter focuses on key elements of meditation. It is a God-given act or a method by which you envision the truthful hope revealed about you and your future. You find that meditation helps you experience the very presence of God. I mean, you will experience God, thought to thought, Spirit to spirit, knowing His will innately as He speaks the language of your mind. Through words, images, flashes of scenes in life that is to come, scenes that are your hope, and your destiny, God will reveal His intent for you. By virtue of its meaning, meditation carries us into a realm where we mutter the positives and proclaim the truth, rehearsing them in our mind, deprogramming the old debilitating thoughts, and instilling the new principles of truth. Philosophically speaking, we actualize what *is* and suspend what *was*.

I included the words "Cold Serenity" in the title for this chapter on winter, the season of meditation, for a specific reason. It was the winter of 1985. I had just relocated to Cleveland, Tennessee, to attend Lee University. I had never experienced living and driving in weather conditions, with temperatures in single digits accompanied by streets covered with snow. I remember this time quite vividly, probably because I had to walk two miles to my first class of the winter semester. I couldn't dig my car out of the snow, and even if I could, I didn't have any snow tires to drive on the iced roads. Needless to say, I wasn't prepared for the challenges of that cold winter.

A newbie in town, and everyone seemed to know it, I walked onto the campus for the first time as a student. As I walked to class that day, with teeth chattering, I questioned God as to why

I chose such a place to attend college. At that moment, a slight fear gripped my heart, so I stopped in front of the library, then on Ocoee Street. There seemed to be a million thoughts that consumed my mind immediately. I was paralyzed with thoughts. Why couldn't I move forward to my class? Was it fear? Was it the cold conditions? Could it be that I was questioning my academic ability? No ... it was fear. Fear of the unknown.

This was the beginning of a new phase in my life. I knew very few people there. It was cold, and I wasn't very impressed with my experiences up to that point. But there, in front of the library, almost immediately following my confrontation with fear, I felt a peace that saturated my entire being. I stood amid those snow-covered streets in a serenity I had never known. At that moment, I knew I was where God wanted me to be. It was as if there was a freshness that permeated the air, filling the lungs of my anticipated daily experiences and breathing life into the barren places of my soul. When I think back, those were pivotal years for me. They will always be in my memory.

Lee University was a place of replanting, a place of nurture at that time in my life. It is located in a city where there is absolutely nothing to do but study. It was the perfect learning environment! No distractions, only those you create for yourself. That statement appropriately describes the winter environment of meditation, which requires your undivided attention. It is that time in your life when you must be willing to stand alone for what you believe to be true.

Meditating helps us to control our life situations

If you do, you will enter into a realm that transcends natural tendencies. You will come into the calm, the peace that passes all natural understanding. Your circumstances, however troubling, will lose potency in this realm. The degree to which you experience this sacred calm is determined by how much of yourself you're willing to unfold. In essence, how much of your *self* are you willing to let go to achieve maximum benefit during your season of meditation? The answer to that question will determine the degree of God's sacred calm to which you will be privy.

In certain parts of the world, the winter season commands a reverent pause in life. Streets are closed; businesses and commerce halt because of the restricted conditions. In relationships, we experience a stillness that restricts the norms of our lives. It is a time when we should reflect, not only in words and verbal discourse, but in the quietness of pondering the richness of what God has revealed and given to us.

At one point in time, the object of our lives was fixed on a wounded mind. Over and over in that wounded mind, our tendencies were to play and replay the failures of our past, reopening sorrow's deep cuts and prolonging the healing process. We allowed bitterness, self-pity, or resentment into the open wounds. Meditation commands a pause in our mental play and playback that points us upward and beyond ourselves. During meditation, we are to simplify and empty our lives of the attachments that can distract us and hinder us from forming a meaningful relationship with the divine One, which is the true objective of life.

In his book *Practicing the Presence*, Joel S. Goldsmith brings depth to the meaning of meditation. He says, "Meditation is an invitation for God to speak to us or to make Himself known to us; it is not an attempt to reach God, since God is omnipresent. The Presence already is. The Presence always is, in sickness or in health, in lack or in abundance, in sin or in purity; the presence of God always and already is. We are not seeking to reach God, but rather to achieve such a state of stillness that the awareness of God's presence permeates us."[11] Goldsmith assures us that we are not alone in any circumstance, but the only venue for unlocking the mind of God into your life is through meditation.

Coming into right relationship with God through prayer and meditation heals the wounded human mind. I have not experienced any relationship in life that brings wholeness to my life and healing to my emotional well-being like the personal relationship I share with God. He has never forsaken me or left me alone. Augustine once said, "My soul is restless until it finds its rest in Thee, O God." I found solace in that statement, but there was a time when I shared the sentiments of Frances Thompson (1859–1907). In his poem titled "The Hound of Heaven," Thompson expressed reluctance toward God's personal bidding. He said,

> I fled Him, down the nights and down the days;
> I fled Him, down the arches of the years;
> I fled Him, down the labyrinthine ways
> Of my own mind; and in the mist of tears
> I hid from Him, and under running laughter.

We must all come to the point where we cease fleeing the pursuing presence of God. We must dry the tears from our eyes and abandon the thoughts that keep us from discovering and believing in something higher and more sufficient than ourselves. It is "In him that we live, and move, and have our being" (Acts 17:28). Our inner, undeniable need for personal significance was created to make us search for Him at the point of our exhausting all natural means. In Him, we find peace, acceptance, and love. Through Him, we find the courage and power to develop into the men and women He intended us to be.

In our time of meditation with Him, we can be freed from the past issues that hindered us and experience a renewed purpose for our lives. Denying the importance of God and His truth, people are left with only their natural abilities and the opinions of others on which to base their lives and personal worth. The results are such that the circumstances around them ultimately control their entire existence and affect how they feel about themselves. Meditation is the key to true peace, clarity, and rest from the toils of life. The practice of meditation enables a person to come out and be separated from the distractions of a fast-paced world. The season of winter is a purifying time of preparing the soil of the mind for the sowing of new seeds of thought. Remember, the secret of meditation is silence: no repetitions, no affirmations, no denials; just the acknowledgment of God's presence. When we do that, we bring the divine presence into our affairs; forgetting the things of this world, we turn within and make contact with the One, whom I comfortably call God—our source.

Meditation is the key to maximizing the clarity and creative potential of our thought-life

I close this chapter with the hope that you've kept an open mind thus far, allowing something fresh to prompt you to begin thinking about your life from a different perspective. There is a great spiritual mystery in all of this. The closer we get to God in meditation, the more He will unfold into our minds. He will unfold the things that are relative to our growth and purpose on the earth. Be challenged by the fact that seasons change, and if we're true to ourselves, the burning desire to be better individuals will challenge us to acknowledge where we are in life and develop appropriately through each season. Don't resist the solitude of your winter season. The peace, clarity, and rest found in this meditative season will prepare your mind for renewal. This is the process of purification and will be discussed in chapter 10.

Meditation was used in relation to a season of separation from relationships during a specific time or season in life. Let me point out, however, that practicing it only during your winter season is not enough. Meditation should be a continuous way of life each day of your life. Carve out moments in your day to acknowledge the presence of the Spirit of God. Never make a move without His inner assurance of supplying us, enriching us, healing us, and bringing us into the fullness of life.

I trust this chapter has impacted your life and stirred up something within you that will encourage you to welcome your winter season of meditation.

10

A Time of Inner Cleansing

That Which Is Mine
Preston Williams II

I die daily a thousand deaths,
Only to triumph life's illusory web.

These deaths within resurrect a new life,
The one tradition conceals, the one that
Precludes my awakening from the
Picture perfect dream.

Arising, I see ahead of me ...
I see forming that which is now
Possible ... happiness ...
A breath without pain ...
My due.

Inner cleansing is much like the above poetic piece. It is the process of coming into your most perfected self. Please don't misunderstand this statement. I did not say that you are perfect, or that you ever will be. But you can be involved in the perfecting process, which is an ongoing venture. Your most perfect self is what you can look back on at the end of your inner cleansing, personal and spiritual empowerment, and the principle of the day's experience, understood and applied to the point of a new level of maturity. This is a day-by-day, moment-by-moment cleansing process for the duration of your life. In this process, there will never be a conclusion of perfection. But it is a process that is understood from the perspective of continuous maturity.

It is continuous, because our capacity for growth and maturity is immeasurable. This alone should stimulate you to explore and develop your personhood each day with a newfound sense of enthusiasm and expectancy. You're privy to the possibility that there's so much more of your true *self* to be discovered and exposed to the world. What's more fascinating is that our capacity potential concurs with the fact that we are created in the image of the One whose measure is limitless. Only He knows our true measure of fulfillment.

Inner cleansing clears away the debris of "life learned" so that "life discerned/revealed" through truth may be developed and nurtured. The previous seasons of exposing, identifying, trimming up, and cutting off have left their debris on the ground of our life. We may even find some lurking impurities in the atmosphere of our mind. Therefore, life's winter season, like the earth's winter season, is a time of final purification before the season of spring.

Meditation prepares us to deal with our internal selves. We are more cognitive of how we've been affected by the exterior and are now focused on those elements of our lives that are true to our real selves. Here are some "power thoughts" I extracted from my past winter seasons. They have been most effective for me as I continue in my life of "becoming." I trust they will do the same for you: (1) Away with generational cloning (*I am not seeking to be like others who were before me, I just want to be me*), (2) Away with the ideals I have no personal connection with (*I have no interest in acting out the ideals of others when I have no personal conviction toward them*), (3) It's time to take time out from unhealthy, unproductive relationships (*I am seeking personal wholeness beyond the influence and affirmation of others*). These three power thoughts may seem so simple, but I dare you to live them out in your personal life! They are guaranteed to bring about positive change for anyone who wholeheartedly embraces them.

My time of inner cleansing resulted from the above personal affirmations. I live my life by them, and because of these affirmations, I am able to appreciate each individual as being unique in his or her own way. This has enabled me to maximize the positive impartial impact I make on the lives of everyone I meet. This should be the goal of persons seeking to free themselves of uncomfortable relationships. Somehow, personal interactions free from preconceived expectations and judgments having no unsubstantiated verdicts transcend the moments you encounter with others. The same applies in life's circumstances: never prejudge their causes or outcomes. Previous bad experiences impart debilitating information in our minds, resulting in the resuscitation of harmful, conditioned reactions in our hearts. This behavior is referred to as respondent conditioning—an innate, involuntary behavior elicited or caused by an antecedent (conditions and traits of one's earlier life).

Inner cleansing remedies these prejudicial innate conditions by filtering your thought-life, stabilizing your confidence, and reenergizing your outlook on life. The following pages will provide a comprehensive study of these. Inner cleansing is an extension of meditation.

Filtering Your Thought-life

Filtering your thought-life involves a basic knowledge of how the mind works. When we understand how the mind works, the filtering process will make sense. It will personally empower us in such a way that we realize our capability to manage information received, opinions shared, and convictions that shape our belief system. A theological and philosophical known fact is that you are who you are, and where you are in life, because of your belief system. The belief system is what we rely on to function in life.

The first step in understanding how your belief system affects the complex dimensions of your thought-life is examination of the thinking process.

Thinking involves the mental manipulation of information. It fosters reasoning, solving problems, making decisions and judgments, and imagining. These are the unseen dimensions of everyday life prior to actual manifestation—everything is created twice—first mentally, then physically. What this means is that the manifestation of anything in life, good or bad, begins with thought. This single truth places your thought-life in a very powerful position of control.

Let us examine the mental complex in order to gain understanding of how it manipulates information, thus controlling life through the power of choice. The mental complex consists of three components: the *conscious mind*, the *subconscious mind*, and the *conscience mind*. The conscious mind handles purposeful or conscious thoughts and the day-to-day decisions. It manages the initial reasoning and logical thinking that require concentration. The subconscious mind is the autopilot of the conscious mind and is responsible for automatically carrying out the finished work of the conscious mind. When the conscious mind has thought through a process and accepted certain norms and values as truth, from that moment on, the subconscious begins to handle decision making at a level that does not require much conscious thought at all.

One good analogy to explain this is driving a car to the same destination each day. It requires less thought and attention to details because of the frequency. Have you ever driven home from work and for a time not paid close attention to where you're going? Instinctively, you safely made all the right turns and arrived at your destination without deliberate attention to the details of your trip. Your subconscious serves the conscious mind and eliminates the necessity to rethink known tasks and values over and over again. The subconscious mind also accesses our belief and value system and makes many decisions at a "sub," or below, conscious level all the time, which is a valuable asset. The conscience mind houses my belief and value systems. It is the reference point by which all things are judged. Our thoughts are channeled through this mental complex, and we function in life by this process of thinking.

Mind filtering involves the deprogramming and maintenance of information that is stored in our mind's autopilot (subconscious). It monitors the intake valve of the mind (conscious), which in turn shapes the seat of our conviction and our passions in life (conscience). The winter season of our lives is a time of cleansing the mental complex so that we are able to function from a more divinely informed position in life. Nothing is more lethal to successful living than contaminated thoughts constantly processed through the mental complex, affecting the way we respond to life. Therefore, we must turn our attention to our thoughts and embrace the concept of inner cleansing. For a more in-depth understanding of how our thoughts filter, allow me to make a comparison to that of air current.

You are who you are and where you are in life because of your belief system

Thoughts are like the wind, and wind is air in a flow or a current. One of the most important attributes of air is its life-sustaining property. Like the flow of air, thoughts flow through our minds, affecting the activity and the sustenance of life. Additionally, air is our source of oxygen, and oxygen is essential to cells, which use this vital substance to liberate the energy needed for cellular activities. As clean air is vital for the liberation of energy, so are clear thoughts for motivation, purposeful activities, and actions toward the fulfillment of destiny. A clean thought-life is an essential element needed in lives for promotion of effective growth and development. Thoughts, like air, are challenged by the impurities that are caught in its flow. These circulate throughout the atmosphere of our minds. We're exposed to these impurities daily, but we should not allow them to consume us physically, mentally, or spiritually.

The study of anatomy and physiology reveals a process that we should treasure as a principle of mental inner cleansing. The physical organs of the respiratory system serve a dual purpose. They deliver oxygen to the circulatory system for transport to all body cells, and they also aid in removing the waste product, carbon dioxide. This process prevents the lethal buildup of carbon dioxide in body tissues. In essence, it is a filtering process that removes dust and all other particles that prohibit your capacity to breathe. Day after day, without the prompting of conscious thought, the respiratory system carries out its life-sustaining activities. If the respiratory system's tasks are interrupted for more than a few minutes, serious, irreversible damage to tissues occurs, failure of all the body systems follow, and death is inevitable.

When we apply the principles of the physical filtering process to our thought-life, we discover that it is equally critical to the life-sustaining activities we're involved in as we engage in the movement and rhythm of life. In previous chapters, we see where truth, the innate voice of God, is our filter. As we read, enfold, and meditate on God's word of truth, it becomes a part of our mental filtering system. It renovates our consciousness, alerting us to possible moral contaminates, perception distorters, and progress prohibitors. We've just learned that if the physical respiratory system's tasks are interrupted, problems occur. Similarly, if our truth filter is interrupted by erroneous philosophy, personal prejudice, or resurrection of the old man's nature and negative influences, our mental and spiritual systems will be affected. Whereas in the physical, irreversible tissue damage may occur, in the mental, renewed application of truth can transform and heal any damage incurred from a breakdown or interruption of known truth principles that have been temporarily abandoned for whatever reasons.

The manifestation of anything in life, good or bad, begins with thought

Like all filters, your thought-life must be checked periodically for any residue. If you're experiencing clouded judgment, you may need to check your mental filter. If you find it difficult to stay focused on purpose-driven activities, you may need to check your mental filter. If you feel like you're on life's treadmill—lots of movement but going nowhere—Amber alert! Check your mental filter! Don't wait for the pending symptoms of a problem, exercise preventive maintenance measures. Take caution in what you embrace as truth, and scrutinize all references concerning you and your life's situations. Remember, you're totally responsible for the choices you make in life. Caution! I have yet to meet the individual who wants to take responsibility for another's failures. One thing is certain though; everyone stands ready to accept at least partial, if not all, credit for your success in life.

Stabilizing Your Confidence

Your confidence equilibrium is another vital element of your forward movement in life; it is a by-product of inner cleansing. Referring to the parallel of the physiology of respiratory filtering, the intake of oxygen and removal of carbon dioxide are the primary functions of the respiratory system. But it plays other important roles in the body. The respiratory system helps to regulate the balance of acid and base in tissues. This is a process that is critical for the normal functioning of cells. It protects the body against disease-causing organisms and toxic substances that gain entrance through inhalation. The balance of confidence is crucial for our mental functioning in the pursuit of destiny. Confidence comes as a by-product of thought filtering. The more clearly you're able to see yourself in the light of truth, the more confident you are in your capacity to follow through with the activities necessary for progress and fulfillment. A stabilized confidence protects against mental *dis-ease-* (meaning uneasiness) causing elements or issues. There is no mistake in my spelling; I deliberately hyphenated the word disease to mean that it really is a disruption of your personal *ease* when your confidence is shattered!

Confidence is an innate empowerment, an inspired breath of life breathed into a desolate soul. Confidence is a renewed hope in life; it is an optimism that is the foundation of releasing latent potential. There was a quote from James Allen in chapter 7. He shared some profound insights on the inner cleansing of thoughts and the basic dynamics of personal confidence. He said, "A man can only rise, conquer, and achieve by lifting up his thoughts … by the right choices and true application of thought, man ascends to the Divine Perfection."

Although we're not perfect within ourselves, one of the goals in life is that we strive for perfection. When the focus of our striving is centered on the destination of transcending our finite, compromised thoughts, I believe we enter into the realm of the divine perfection. It is in that realm we find our confidence stabilized and our renewed selves poised for fearless movement toward our destiny in life. Nothing is more exhilarating than the conquest of life's challenges in the spirit of confidence and everything that comes along with the results of its victories. One biblical writer said, "Cast not away your confidence which has great reward" (Hebrews 10:35).

Confidence comes as a by-product of thought filtering

The winter season is a time of solitude, which allows an individual to filter their beliefs and perceptions. It is one of the most valuable time spans one will ever spend. Those are moments that will have a most profound effect in that person's life. If properly utilized, one can remake one's life and present it to the world with unshakable confidence. To remake yourself for success and fulfillment of destiny, you must reconstruct your thinking to include the confidence factor. There's a psychological principle that says, "To think confidently, act confidently." Psychologist Dr. George W. Crane said in his famous book *Applied Psychology* (Chicago: Hopkins Syndicate, Inc., 1950), "Remember, motions are the precursors of emotions. You can't control the latter directly but only through your choice of motions or actions. ... Go through the proper motions each day and you'll soon begin to feel the corresponding emotions."[12]

I equate this statement to reflect proper motions as an individual moving in the rhythm of their destiny. It is the divine act of being drawn into the uncharted waters of life and responding with personal movement that defies previously limited logic. Confidence begins to strengthen each time movement is made, and it proves to be the antithesis to the wall of fear, which is being chipped away in direct proportion to your action(s). During your journey in life, you will face fear. Uncontrolled fear will cause you to abort your goals, purposes, and forward movement in life. Many people cheat themselves out of the peace and prosperity that belong to them because they fail to take action.

Inner cleansing is the combination of renewed thoughts and actions. According to Dr. Crane, confident thinking is a by-product of confident acting. Mental confidence is nurtured by acting on what you know to be true. *Acts* cures *fear*. To move into your new realm of "becoming," it is imperative that you isolate your fear and take constructive action. Inactivity strengthens fear and destroys confidence. Your old, inferior thought-life will desire to take over and move you back to your previous defective actions or ways of responding to life. *Don't do it! You must learn how to manage and control your thinking, control your confidence level, and become focused so that you're operating at an optimum response level to your everyday circumstances.*

Think about the physiological effects of action on your confidence level. I challenge you in this area, because I believe that each individual must initiate, participate, and involve themselves in the divine plan for their life. Your confidence development is dependent on action. For example, you actually feel more like smiling if you make yourself smile. Your emotions will respond very quickly to the feedback signals of your posture. It is difficult to cry and feel depressed while engaging a big grin on your face. It is equally difficult to feel disempowered when you are walking as boldly as a king of a great kingdom. You must begin thinking and acting on the level you'd like to attain. Here are four points that you should activate or employ to stabilize your confidence.

1. Remember, action is the key to nurturing confidence! The Bible says that, "faith without works is dead" (James 2:26). Read your Bible, reflect on its truth, and practice its principles.
2. Intentionally meditate on thoughts that offer affirmations and thoughts that edify you as a person of purpose. Reject self-destructive thoughts that could develop into "mental terrorists," terrorizing your emotional well-being, weakening your confidence.
3. Put people in their proper perspective. Never assume you're less significant than anyone else. God is no respecter of persons, and we are all considered His remarkable creation (Acts 10:34).
4. Develop sensitivity toward your inner voice, the Spirit that connects you with truth. It is your new voice of reason. Take the time to be still, be quiet, and listen.

It is important to note that no one is born with confidence. Confidence is acquired or developed. People who seem to radiate confidence in every situation in life have had to develop that. Life will present you with the most unique circumstances to assist in your development of this needed characteristic of destiny. As I have admonished you in previous chapters, don't avoid the opportunity to grow, and don't avoid the perfecting process. The process of developing confidence is no exception.

Reenergizing Your Life's Outlook

Your ability to grasp and cast vision is also a by-product of the effectiveness of your filtering process. Hopefully by now you're transcending old methodology and locking into a renewed pattern of thinking. Vision is so precious that one must properly appropriate it with confidence and clarity. Inner cleansing is a part of bringing clarity to your future outlook or vision. According to Dr. I. V. Hilliard, "Where there is clarity of vision, there is immediate acceleration toward a known goal." He continues by saying, "Have you ever been driving toward a known destination, a friend's home, work or a different city, and fog descended on the road? You immediately begin to decelerate to take into account that lack of vision. You navigate cautiously to compensate for the vision obstruction caused by the fog. When the fog lifts, what happens? That's right! You immediately begin to accelerate toward your destination."[13] Inner cleansing clears away the fog of life, allowing acceleration toward your purpose in life.

Once the fog has lifted, you're able to see clearly the path you must take in life. Then you must internalize the vision, or the foresight. Internalizing creates an intangible, fiery energy inside you that can only be quenched by accomplishing what you saw in a systematic approach. Internalizing definitely stimulates your internal functions to move you in the direction toward achieving your desired goal. I am always brought to a moment of pause and humbled when I reflect on my life and see what I've been allowed to accomplish.

If you had asked me fifteen years ago where I thought I would be today, my reply would in no way reflect where I am now. At that time, I allowed others to dictate my worth, and I'd fallen prey or victim to their opinions. It was only after I'd detached myself from the people and the positions I assumed measured or defined who I was and what I should become that I discovered my true self and destiny. For the first time in my life, I had no organizational backing, no family "name" to depend on, and no peer group to encourage me. My true life was being measured in a balance, and everything I embraced would now be scrutinized. One huge revelation I came to terms with during my inner cleansing season was that I should never have allowed popular opinions and widely accepted worldly philosophies to dictate my place in this world.

Where there is clarity of vision, there is immediate acceleration toward a known goal

Here are some simple principles I learned during that time. Never define or measure your vision within the realm of selfish ambition. You were given life to impact the lives of others. Never become "status" driven; this should never be the motivating factor of pursuing vision. If your vision for life is measured by status, then your upkeep could be your downfall. Nothing in life is more frustrating and exhausting than attempting to maintain a status-driven lifestyle. Vision should never be attempted because of status, and certainly not preserved by it. In order to grasp the true spirit and concept of vision, you must start with its origin; vision is buried in purpose. Vision, by virtue of its biblical meaning, is *a guiding, redemptive revelation*. It is the provision by which you're rescued from a depraved way of life. Vision places you on your correct course toward fulfilling purpose in your life and the lives of others.

Inner cleansing emphasizes the pursuit of purpose rather than the idle contentment of fate or the selfish pursuit of status-driven vision. Without purity in the pursuit of purpose, life becomes an endless string of activities with little or no significance. As was stated in the introduction of this book, purpose answers the question of the "why" of life. Like a rider on a rocking horse, life without purity of purpose makes much motion but has no meaningful progress. Purity of purpose also gives us the confidence spoken of. It assures us that what we are doing is the right thing. With a filtered thought-life and a stabilized confidence, you create a mental environment for an energized, driven vision that grips your soul with passion. What was once impossible in your previous mind-set is now possible, and your mind begins to open up. When you have tasted the manna of possibilities, it is difficult to settle for impossibilities.

We encounter so many experiences that dim our outlook on life and squelch our enthusiasm to reach for the brighter stars in the night skies of our lives. The winter season in our lives allows us the opportunity to catch a glimpse of what we're to seek after ... to get a taste of walking in the realm of possibilities. The separation and time out from the confusing voices that once resounded daily can bring healing to your mind and free it to dream the impossible dreams. The purification of thought reenergizes the visionary, and the hidden hope resurfaces. It will feel as if someone called you forth from the dead, a resurrection of sorts, and life becomes an anticipated adventure rather than an ill-fated existence.

11

Identifying the Elements of Your True Self

Self-Realization
Preston Williams II

Looking into a mirror who did I expect to see?
With conclusive confidence I assumed … me!
Analyzing my thoughts, my soul, who did I think me to be?
One of compassion, natural instincts, and a zest
For living with a basic philosophy.

Searching my human spirit, what insightful
Discovery … revelation would there be?
Self-realization, something to set me free.
Am I the soul stirring emotions and
Philosophical impressions I feel?

Reality of self lies deep within the
Threefold nature of creation. I am not
Who I thought I was; I am not who others
Think I am. I am a human spirit possessing a
Soul … housed in the reflective image you and I see.

I can never hide myself from me. I see what others
May never see. I know what others may never know;

I can never fool myself.
I have to live with myself and so,
I want to be true to myself to know …
How to be pure, self-respecting, and
Conscience free … embracing the real me …
The hidden person of the heart.

Is it possible to accurately define one's self by the reflection one sees in the mirror each day? Can we by historical or biographical experience define who we are in the scheme of life? I don't think so. "Read no history, only biography, for that is life without theory," is advice from Benjamin Disraeli. Within these words lies some amount truth, but life without theory still fails to bring true definition to the "self" who lives the life. I'm not convinced that our experiences define us. I believe our experiences are subject to the choices we make and are, to varying degrees, dependent on others who influence us (for example, peer pressure), who are also in need of self-realization. Food for thought, apart from our experiences and influences, who are we?

The basic needs are food, shelter, and clothing. Along with the basic needs in life, there is the desire to be understood and accepted. We all find ourselves in this position at one point or another in life. This is where the loss of true selves begins. I believe it is more important that we know and accept ourselves first. When we know our true selves, we should be able to enter into any relationship and fit in with a healthy sense of purpose. This is important, because we are not then subject to the reshaping of others around us. Unfortunately, this is seldom the case. Humanity thirsts for external recognition and affirmation. How tragic to expect others to know and accept us when we ourselves are unsure of who we are. Because of this expectation, let me draw your attention to what I term *social-schizophrenia*. Social-schizophrenia is when an individual lives two lives.

There are two sides of you: the *visible* you and the *real* you. The visible you is the "you" that others know. We know intuitively from our experiences how to act and speak in order to fit in with different peer groups or situations. In behavioral therapy, this behavior is classified as *masking*. The visible you is the external you that others see and know. It is rarely the *real* you. We have learned to speak and act in ways that allow us to cope with our world and peacefully coexist. We work hard to project a certain image of ourselves to others. We are who we are in our minds first, before we speak or act. Our speech and actions are the result of our thinking. Scripture tells us, "The heart is deceitful above all things and beyond cure. Who can understand it?" (Jeremiah 17:9). To protect your self-image you kid, trick, and fool ourselves into believing the *visible* you is real.[14] I believe we all can identify with that.

Much of humanity is lost in the sea of popular opinion. Too many are defeated in life because popular opinion causes them to look at the wrong things. All they see are the causes and effects of external demands. They are defeated because they allow others to affect their feelings. I often say, "I'm not moved by what I see. I'm not moved by what I feel. I'm moved only by what I believe." The outward person is seen, but the inward person is the hidden, unseen self, the real you. If you are at a time in your life where you are in search of your true self, then you must begin the process of dying to the false identity to which you are accustomed. The person created from all sides: family, friends, media, and society as a whole.

The world is filled with people wandering aimlessly in the midst of life; people who have no grip on their true identity. The opinions of others are more important to them than the way they should see themselves. On the other extreme, there are some people who are so full of themselves or overly confident. They tend to project an "I've arrived" attitude. They, too, possess a life just as fragmented, and they live life under a façade that eventually proves to be an exhausting responsibility to maintain.

Apart from our experiences and influences, who are we?

The winter season of life's experiences is the ideal time to engage in self-realization. It is during such times that we discover who we really are, outside of what we think we know about ourselves. We find that throughout life, we blocked our own self-realization and, in doing so, nurtured an annoying personal disharmony. Have you ever felt inwardly distant from yourself? Are you trying to accept the person others deem you to be, but at the same time, struggling because innately you know that you not what they see? Deep inside, you sense there is something about you that you've not acknowledged, and intuitively, you know that something within you is trying to connect with the only you that you know.

The conflict comes with the fact that some individuals experience life from a one-dimensional perspective, which incorporates the senses. If they can't see it, touch it, taste it, smell it, and hear it, in their minds, it is not relevant. We live in a world that demands sense-realm evidence. This will always limit our capacity to develop, even in the sphere of defining who we are. In the book *Counseling and the Nature of Man*, Drs. Frank and Paul Meier state, "Man has a nature that can best be described by using the word *comprehensive*. In other words, he is a physical, psychological, and spiritual creature, and all of these dimensions are interrelated. … Man is a whole. What affects him physically affects him psychologically and spiritually as well."[15] We see where a physical impairment can lead to psychological and spiritual issues. Later in the discussion, we will see that these dimensions are not only interrelated but also interdependent. In the theological halls of academia, these dimensions are termed spirit, soul, and body—(spiritual, psychological, and physical).

As we explore the true identity of "self," I ask you to expand your mind beyond the obvious—the sense-realm. I also ask you to embrace some simple, yet profound, elements of truth.

Together, we shall draw insight from two schools of thoughts: the theological and the philosophical. In the lives of the seekers of truth, the winter season of reflection and pause sharpens their sensitivity to acknowledge, even for brief intervals, dimensions of self that are unseen and usually ignored. The tri-nature of mankind has always been a mystery to me. It is difficult to discuss the "elements of your true self" without realizing that the physical self is only the house for the true "you." In a time where so much emphasis is placed on the body, the physical beauty, it's no wonder many individuals identify themselves with the "man in the mirror" mentality. This concept is the biggest lie embraced by humanity! I realized this one day as I was about to enjoy a nice cold beverage while preparing for my study time.

I took a bottle of Coke from the refrigerator and a glass from the cabinet. Like anyone, I identify Coke by the unusual shape of the bottle. Growing up, we guys would equate a woman's beautiful body shape with that of the Coke bottle. Many of you may smile at that comment, but you know it is true. The symmetry of the woman's body was paralleled with the Coke bottle because of their shapely similarities. As I opened the bottle of Coke and began to pour the substance into my glass, it occurred to me that I had made a big misjudgment. The bottle was not the Coke. The moment I poured the content of the bottle into the glass, the bottle became an empty, shapely container. The true identity of the Coke, therefore, was the substance that was transferred to a differently shaped glass. Truly, there was a distinct difference between the container and the content.

We are who we are in our minds first— before we speak or act

The foundational thought I would like for you to extract from this chapter is *never confuse the container with the content*. In essence, never confuse "who" you are with "what" you're in. This is such a common dilemma in our day. The need to be known innately for whom we really are rather than what we are externally is vast. I have counseled many couples, both married and unmarried, who are frustrated with their partner simply because the relationship has no personal depth. Their relationship never grew beyond the exterior, physical, sense-realm attraction. For both sexes, it is important to come to terms with the fact that pursuing someone for outward beauty alone is apt to cause deceit. What is considered a "perfect ten" today may not be ten years from now. Love should be channeled toward a truer personhood, the real person, the attitude, character, inner spirit being; all the essentials that will not change. In identifying the true you, it is tantamount that you understand this basic truth. Your *body* is not the whole of who you are. Further on, we'll establish the existence of two other very important dimensions of you, the *spirit* and the *soul*.

The term "trichotomism" is a popular view in conservative Protestant circles. It is the belief that a human being is composed of three elements. The first element is the physical body, something humans have, which is common to animals and plants. The second part is the soul. This is the psychological element, the basis of reason, emotion, social interrelatedness, and the like. Animals, like human beings, possess these two elements, but there is a distinguishing factor that human beings possess and animals don't. It is not a more complex and advance soul, but a third element, namely, a spirit. This religious element enables humans to perceive spiritual matters and respond to spiritual stimuli. It is the seat of the spiritual qualities of the individual, where personality traits reside in the soul.[16]

A good portion of trichotomism is credited to ancient Greek metaphysics. Except for an occasional explicit reference, however, the influence of the Greek philosophers is not readily apparent. Actually the major foundation of trichotomism is in certain Scripture passages that either enumerate three components of human nature or distinguishes between the soul and the spirit. A primary text is 1 Thessalonians 5:23, "May God Himself, the

God of peace, sanctify you through and through. May your whole spirit, soul, and body be kept blameless."[17] Briefly, man's threefold nature is:

(1) **Spirit**—The dimension of man that deals with the spiritual realm. The part of man that knows God.
(2) **Soul**—The dimension of man that deals with the mental realm. Man's intellect. The sensibilities and will. The part that thinks and reasons.
(3) **Body**—The dimension of man that deals with the physical realm. The house in which we live.

I want you to begin to think of yourself in a new light. Don't think of yourself as just a physical being. Simply put, think of yourself as a spirit who possesses a soul and lives in a body.[18] The body is the seat and means of our present life, but not a necessary part of the spirit/soul person. Rather, it is the origin through which our spirit/soul person gathers sensations and expresses itself. At death, it is the death of the body; the spirit/soul person lives on, quite successfully. It leaves the material body, but lives on and enters a new sphere of existence. To further validate this truth, Scripture affirms the separation, "To be absent from the body is to be present with the Lord" (2 Corinthians 5:8*a*, paraphrased).

Even in the Hindu religion, they embrace the body as being only a vessel that carries the true individual. The following is from a sacred Hindu treatise called the Upanishads:

Even as a caterpillar, when coming to the end of a blade of grass, reaches out to another blade of grass and draws itself over to it, in the same way the Soul, leaving the body and Unisom behind, reaches out to another body and draws itself over to it.

That Soul is not this, it is not that it is unseizable, for it cannot be seized; it is indestructible, for it cannot be destroyed; unattached, for it does not attach itself; is unbound, does not tremble, is not injured."

If such emphasis is placed on the spirit/soul (true self) and the body is the abandoned aspect of existence in the end, then why the obsession with the body? Clearly, the body is a tool of present life existence and is to be properly managed, but it is not to be worshipped, and we are not to extract from it our definition of true self-identification.

Understanding trichotomism is important because of the present crisis in human self-understanding. You, like many others in this world, struggle to discover who you truly are. The quest for identity has always been a part of the normal process of maturation. The quest for identity is also involved in forming one's independent outlook on life and forming one's own values and goals. Knowing one's true self (the human spirit) is crucial to mankind's emotional, spiritual, and social stability. Understanding this single need opens the door to understanding our actions and attitudes. The attempt to change behavior is a waste unless you truly understand your innate self. All the previous seasons until this point are the tools God uses to prepare the soil of our minds to receive this one truth.

Human Spirit
Preston Williams II

Who am I?
I am not who you think I am
I am not what you think I am
Only I know.

Perception is not universal truth;
It is individual hypothesis,
Yourself versus myself evaluations.
So ... who am I?

Am I a multitude of perceptions?
Am I a race?
Am I a culture?
Am I a people?

I am that I am
I am neither black nor white,
Asian or European.

I am a spirit of love
Emanating from the mouth of God;
Colorless, and global,
Trapped in multicolored flesh called
Man, woman: whose selfish ambitions
Blind them, allowing tomorrow's
Uncertainty to consume them.

I am you …
Acknowledge me …
Identify me …
Release me …
And change your world!

I wrote this poetic piece in 1992, during the eve of my winter season in life. I, too, was searching for the person of destiny, who had evaded my sense of "knowing" until those pivotal months of being alone with my thoughts and God. It was a time of redefining and releasing the real me. I had to realize that my life would have no value to anyone if I wasn't true to my self about myself. I chose to embrace the real me … the inward person … and then to release that person to the world. Some things in life are optional, while others are not. You have the choice to reject new information that will open a new world of experiences for you, or grab it and flow with the movement of destiny. If you choose to reject your true identity the consequences are clear:

1. You will find yourself sitting on the sideline of life watching, when you could be in the game.
2. You will lose authenticity as an individual. You will continue in the social-schizophrenic syndrome, another term for *hypocrisy*.
3. You will be poorly prepared for the unique challenges in life that were tailored for the person of destiny you were predestined to be.

If you happen to be one of those individuals who feel like you must continue in the façade of life, that it is not necessary to challenge the person you've now come to know as the masked you and the only you others are comfortable knowing, then I encourage you to read on. Keep an open mind; I believe you might just change your opinion. There is so much for you to gain by identifying with your hidden person, your soul and spirit. As I conclude chapter 11, I'll share a thought-provoking literary piece from Kahlil Gibran, a Lebanese poet, philosopher, and artist. In his book *The Prophet*, Gibran had this to say about knowing your self in a piece titled "Self Knowledge":

And a man said, Speak to us of Self Knowledge.
And he answered, saying:
Your hearts know in silence the secrets
Of the days and nights.
But your ears thirst for the sound of
Your heart's knowledge.
You would know in words that which
You have always known in thought.
You would touch with your fingers the
Naked body of your dreams.

And it is well you should.
The hidden well-spring of your soul must
Needs rise and run murmuring to the seas;
And the treasure of your infinite depths
Would be revealed to your eyes.
But let there be no scales to weigh your
Unknown treasure;
And seek not the depths of your knowledge
With staff or sounding line.
For self is a sea boundless and measureless.

Say not, "I have found the truth," but
Rather, I have found a truth."
Say not, "I have met the soul walking
Upon my path."
For the soul walks upon all paths.
The soul walks not upon a line, neither
Does it grow like a reed.
The soul unfolds itself, like a lotus of
Countless petals.[19]

12

Rising Above Fate
to Walk in Destiny

Yet they, believe me, who await
No gifts from chance, have conquered fate.

—Matthew Arnold

Chapter 12 comprises the conclusion of the winter season as well as the other grooming seasons: summer and fall. Winter purifies and positions us for the awaited season of prosperity. It represents the final process before springtime. Spring is the season of birthing; a coming forth of sorts. I chose "Rising Above Fate to Walk in Destiny' as the final chapter of the winter season because I am passionate about challenging the twenty-first-century mind-set that embraces "fate" as their standard of living. Life is too precious to entrust its fulfillment to chance. The spring season demands that we approach it with a planning, participating, and anticipating mind-set so that we experience its maximum benefits.

I know how hard it is to erase the probability of fate operating in life. I equally know how easy it is to take the escape route from personal responsibility. Destiny requires something from you— fate does not. I certainly empathize with someone who is going through what might seem, or appear to be, the toughest period in their entire life. I have been through such a season. At one point

139

I felt like giving up. It is during this period that the lure of fate's temptation is strongest, and you want to give in to thinking that you might as well let fate dictate the next consequence in your life. Though I share your feelings, I will not allow you to keep thinking this way. I must challenge you, be encouraged. Here is the challenge: I overcame the seduction of fate's persuasion, and if I did it, anyone can do it! Fundamentally, I transcended fate to walk in my destiny in life; since then, I have never been the same.

Fatalism and *destiny* were discussed in the introduction of this book. These concepts will now be revisited. We go through seasons in our lives that sometimes seem so wasteful and unnecessary. So much so, that when it is all said and done, we're left with this tiresome feeling that questions the why of life. Not understanding why we go through what we go through is a heart-wrenching experience. Sometimes the frustration of life is so burdensome there is the tendency to curse the fact that we were ever born. The search for understanding life's ups and downs is endless and in many cases, futile. Like the dry, dusty throat of a thirsty man lost in a desert, we reach for so many solutions and philosophies that we assume will quench our thirst. To our dismay, we find ourselves drinking the dust of disillusionment. Empty and disillusioned, we throw up our hands in defeat, resort to a life of mere existence, and adopt the attitude of *que sera sera*—whatever will be will be. In theological circles, this attitude or philosophy is described as fatalism. This philosophy of fatalism does not encourage understanding, nor does it enforce the pursuit of purpose. Fatalism implies that we are all subject to fate, that is, life without the benefit of personal choice, without our cooperation and intentional pursuit of known/revealed purpose. To understand destiny is to cherish the fact that your life has been predetermined or predestined. When you do this, you must also accept another fact: nothing occurs in life without reason or purpose. Without proper direction, we live our lives never knowing the purpose or reason for our experiences—

whether good or bad. Knowing and understanding the reason for these experiences bring ease to the pressures of life and place all events in their proper perspectives. Proper perspective may be interpreted to mean the view in which an idea or experience fits and brings completeness, ease, and understanding.

It is impossible to discuss the subjects, destiny, and fate without including free will, a most important component that bridges the gap between these two schools of thought. Free will is the deciding element that either empowers you to transcend fate and enter into the realm of "walking in destiny" or causes surrender to the call of fate and subject yourself to *chance*. So what is free will? Free will is the power or ability of the human mind to choose a course of action or make a decision without being subject to restraints imposed by antecedent causes, necessity, or divine predetermination. An implemented freewill act is, itself, a cause, not an effect; it is beyond causal sequence or the law of causality. The question of human beings' ability to determine their actions is important in philosophy, particularly in metaphysics, ethics, and theology. Generally, the extreme doctrine in which freedom of the will is affirmed is termed libertarianism. Its opposite, determinism, is the doctrine that human action is not willed freely but rather the result of such influences as passions, desires, physical conditions, and external circumstances beyond the individual's control.

Destiny requires something from you—fate does not

It is my belief that there is a healthy balance between the two theories. To support the libertarianism view is to say that you're the master of your fate without the guidance of a divine plan. On the other hand, to embrace the determinism view is to say that we are all pawns of the universe without the privilege of choice (fate). Millard J. Erickson asserts, "Fate is seen as blind forces, but even then they are forces over which individuals have no influence. This is basically a pessimistic view that pictures people as being crushed by a world that is either hostile or at best indifferent to their welfare and needs. The result is helplessness, or futility."[20] When any individual attempts to disavow responsibility for their life's choices, I consider it improper and a sign of immaturity.

Through the years, in various counseling sessions, I've experienced the following excuses from some of my clients who were simply trying to avoid personal responsibility for dilemmas they found themselves in. A common excuse is genetic conditioning: "I can't control my behavior. It's in my genes. I inherited it from my father." Another is psychological conditioning: "I was raised that way. I can't help being the way I am." Or social conditioning: "When I was growing up, I didn't have a chance. There was no opportunity to get an education." All of these are what Erickson describes as "examples of what existentialism calls 'inauthentic existence,' unwillingness to accept personal responsibility."[21] This failure to exercise one's freedom is a denial of the fundamental dimension of human nature and more so, a denial of one's humanity. Similarly, any effort to deprive others of their freedom of choice is wrong, whether it be through slavery, a totalitarian government, an excessively regulative democracy, or a manipulative social style.

As we approach the process of transcending fate to walk in destiny, I believe with all of my heart that this is where the balance lies. We are beings made in the image of God, having not originated through a chance process of evolution but through a conscious, purposeful act of God. Therefore, human existence lies in the intention of the Supreme Being. This is the foundation on which to pursue destiny. There is a predetermined intent for our lives. We must choose to acknowledge and accept our partnership with God in fulfilling our reason for being. Our lives are innately incomplete when we try to find meaning from regarding ourselves and our happiness as the highest of all values. We fail miserably when we attempt to find happiness, fulfillment, or satisfaction by seeking it directly. Our significance and worth is tied to, and has been conferred on us by, a higher source. We are fulfilled only when we seek, serve, and love that higher being. At that point, we step over the threshold of fate and enter into the realm of assigned *personal destiny*.

To understand destiny is to cherish the fact that your life has been predetermined or predestined

Personal destiny is the "why" of your "being." In modern society, there is a relentless pursuit of success toward personal goals that have not been aligned with the supreme intent. This has led to very unfortunate results. Among them are divorce, suicide, violence, white-collar crimes, emotional depression, and most of all, an inner feeling of helplessness and hopelessness. The reason there's no real understanding or clarity of personal destiny. There is either reliance on fate—whatever happens, happens, or battle with living up to someone else's definition of who they are and why they are. I believe fate is also when we allow others to determine our destiny for us without our input, whether it is a parent, spouse, boss, or society as a whole. Entering into the realm of your personal destiny requires you to be the "you" that has been revealed through the previous seasons of refinement.

You are unique; become familiar with this uniqueness. One Greek philosopher alerts us by saying, "Know thyself." When you find the treasure of uniqueness inside yourself, fate will no longer have a valid voice in your life. Then you will have opened a door to the depths of your true being, and destiny will whisper your name. Listen to Solomon, king of Israel, as he expounds on this truth, "The purposes of a man's heart are deep waters, but a man of understanding draws them out" (Proverbs 20:5). And when that happens, let nothing or no one prevent you from becoming and doing all that you were born to be and do. Pursue it with all of your passion.

In earlier chapters, we saw destiny and purpose used interchangeably. For clarity, I will do so as the need arises. Walking in purpose with a sense of unyielding passion is paramount to your success in life. As Myles Monroe states, "It [destiny] is the only source of meaning." Without purpose, life is an experience or a haphazard journey that results in frustration, disappointment, and failure. Without purpose, life is subjective, or it is a game of trial and error that is ruled by environmental influences and immediate circumstances. Likewise, in the absence of purpose, time has no meaning, energy has no reason, and life has no precision.[22] He claims that, "Consummating that purpose does not just happen as a by-product of life ... you are responsible for the intentional fulfillment of your purpose so the world may benefit from your contribution."[23] In essence, you have the responsibility of intentionally participating in the fulfillment of the plan of destiny in your life.

There are three elements of intentional participation that will be crucial to your crossing over the threshold of fate and walking in destiny: (1) intentional participation through preparation, (2) intentional participation through biblical meditation, and (3) intentional participation through practicing.

Intentional Participation Through Preparation

Fate is synonymous with *chance*. If chance were a valid operation in life, even then, it is said that, "Chance favors the prepared mind." By now you should have a clear vision of what you're to do with your life. Now is the time for preparation. Preparation is the number-one prerequisite for the journey toward your destiny. Preparation involves educational, emotional, and relational refinement. So what are you refining? You are refining old methods of operations, obsolete information, and relational hang-ups. Moreover, you must begin to expand yourself educationally by committing yourself to continuous development and refinement of your skills through a relevant program of study. This can be achieved at an institution of higher learning, or you can engage in disciplined, independent, personal reading to sharpen your knowledge base. Outdated information and old methods of operation should be replaced immediately. Keep an open mind. Always assume that what you've learned is not all there is to know ... be teachable. Your relationships should be tailored toward your destiny. Choose your associations wisely; connect with dream sharers not dream destroyers. Maintain the highest standard of integrity; integrate your words, feelings, actions, and thoughts into wholeness.

Intentional Participation Through Biblical Meditation: Verbalization, Visualization, and Internalization

The word meditation maybe defined as to mutter, to practice beforehand, to envision. There are three components of biblical meditation: verbalization, visualization, and internalization. Decide what you need to change and what you want to be like afterward. These changes should be in agreement with your purpose in life. Write this down with as many graphic details as possible. Then begin to *verbalize* your life's objectives with confidence. Share them with other dreamers with like minds toward fulfilling their destiny. When this is done, several dynamic things take place. Firstly, words create images, so when we speak God's intent for our lives, we are able to get a mental picture of His will for us. Secondly, to speak affirmatively concerning God's intent for our lives releases faith into the situation and triggers divine assistance.

Visualization is sometimes referred to as imaging. This enables you to see or envision the object of meditation. Visualization must have a reference. It is the formation of complete, detailed mental pictures of life situations. Remember the biblical reference of Abraham recorded in the book of Genesis 13:14–16. This is a prime example of God training His created beings to cooperate with His plan for their lives. If God's plan of land possession and prosperity for Abraham was independent of his wife, Sarah, and himself, then God would not have instructed him so carefully on how to receive and possess the promise. God instructed Abraham to do three things. Firstly, to see (envision) the land of promise (Genesis 13:14–16). Secondly, to use his imagination on the stars and sands of the seashore and attach faces to each star and sand particle to create an image in Abraham's mind of the nation that would come forth from his wife and himself ... "So shall thy seed be." Thirdly, to change his name from Abram to Abraham. His new name, Abraham, meant "father of many nations."

Abraham was now calling those things that were not as though they were (Romans 4:17). This caused a release of divine power. Furthermore, this release of power created the potential for success within Abraham to bring about God's intended plan. The ability to look into the future is possible and easier if there is a model of what you desire. Think of a person who is a model of your dream, and envision yourself in that position. When formed in combination with spiritual resources, these pictures are so pure and clear that they are embedded into your conscious mind. A quick flashback to chapter 10 reminds us that the conscious is where these mental pictures create an energy that will empower us to obtain and use resources far beyond what would normally be available to us. Internalization is intertwined with participation through practice.

Intentional Participation Through Practicing

The third component, *internalization*, is the appropriate corresponding action and emotion or affection that anchors the meditation experience. Knowing how to manage your emotions during mediation is essential to your success in this spiritual experience. Internalization is part of the process to help crystallize the vision of the result of your desire. It is a dynamic process of acting out the desire at the level of your faith.[24] I remember having the desire to go back to college to obtain my degree; I was in my late thirties. The voice of my past began to discourage me; fate, excuses, and the like were clouding my goal.

I used these participation principles to guide me through to a clearer vision of where I wanted to be. I remember pulling up a Web site with photos of a college graduation ceremony. I printed a photo of a gentleman wearing his Ph.D. regalia. There he was, standing on that podium, adorned in his long doctoral robe with the three doctor's bars on each sleeve. The dark blue hood draped him with academic distinction. His four-pointed tam and hanging golden tassel complemented his attire. What I did then, I never told a soul until now. You may laugh, I laughed too at first. Yes, I printed out that photo and made a copy of a head-shot picture of myself. Next, I pasted the head shot onto the picture, over the actual gentleman's head. There I was, at his graduation, in his graduation attire, and on his podium receiving his degree!

I then made sufficient space on the wall in my home office to accommodate all three degrees I would receive in the future. Each day I looked at the picture with my head pasted to it in that Ph.D. commencement photo, and I mentally envisioned all three degrees hanging on my wall. I verbalized it, visualized it, and internalized it. Several years later, everything I visualized and internalized came into fruition. Today I have my Ph.D. in Christian counseling and psychology, am vice president at-large of the university I attended, and publishing my fourth book. Dreams really do come true when you transcend fate and walk in the rhythm of your destiny.

Part 3, chapter 12 closes out the winter season and moves us toward the springtime of our life's experience. It is necessary that I emphasize the importance of prayer throughout your entire life, regardless of the season you find yourself sojourning. There is nothing mystical and super-spiritual about prayer that is beyond your grasp. Prayer is simply your quiet-time conversations with God. It is the personal interaction between the source of life and you. With the tool of prayer, you spiritually cover your life's pursuits, submitting them for the approval of the divine. Prayer performs two vital functions. Firstly, you transcend the cares of life and enter into the presence of God. In His presence, you discover that God's love for ideas, creativity, and vision places His energy into your endeavors.

We bask in the feeling of His fond assistance, and we walk in destiny with the full assurance of His provisions and protection. I believe that even Bach, the great composer, used his music as a source of intimate communication with God. It is the combination of a prayer and a praise. Johann Sebastian Bach was the zenith of the composers emerging from the Reformation period. Inscribing his scores with the letters S.D.G.—*Soli Deo Gloria*, "To the Glory of God alone"—Bach wove the words and chords of music in a conscious effort to please and exalt the God from whom his gifts came.

Secondly, prayer changes *you*. As I have said in previous chapters, we all have aspects of our lives that need adjustment and correction. Many times the greatest hindrance to the accomplishments we envision is ourselves. It's this contact with God through prayer that allows us to be cleansed. I am a certified behavior consultant, and I believe in the benefits of psychology and its importance in bringing resolve to the lives of hurting and disillusioned individuals. But I am also a Christian and value the eternal benefits of theology. In my counseling sessions, I encourage a wide range of reading materials that will assist my clients in their process of resolution. The Bible is among these reading materials. I believe it to be the universal truth of God, the infinite mind. I believe there is a healthy balance to be reached as we attempt to heal the ills of our world.

Charles Colson said it best in his book *The Body*. He said, "Without the message (Truth) we are simply offering our own brand of therapy. And therapy can only modify behavior. It is the gospel (good news of Truth) that transforms character. The object or focus is not to make people able to live with themselves; it is to make them able to live with God."[25] When we pray, having aligned ourselves with the gospel of truth, whatever indiscretions these are in our lives, from the least to the greatest, are gathered in the loving hands of a caring God and cast into the sea of forgetfulness, never to be remembered anymore. Whatever the source of the grit in our lives, prayer will wash it out and make us ready to function at maximum potential. Prayer is my greatest resource in my day-to-day challenges. It is my only true source of personal therapy and final resolve.

Prayer is simply your quiet-time conversations with God

Moving into your realm of destiny requires an intimate relationship with your higher source. Whether or not you believe in personal destiny does not change the fact that destiny is real. And whether or not you believe in God, the higher source does not change the fact that He "is and always will be." He is a rewarder of those who diligently seek him and his truth (Hebrews 11:6*b*). Hear the words of Homer:

> No man of woman born,
> Coward or brave, can shun his destiny.
>
> —Homer, *Iliad*, VI

What a powerful phrase of persistence! I believe destiny is a pending and resounding voice throughout our lives, awaiting our ears to hear and our hearts to yield to His beckoning call. Approach your spring season with the resolve to abandon the grip of fate, and walk in your destiny as the providential hand of God escorts you through life to accomplish all that He has ordained for you.

PART IV
Spring: The Season of Renewal

Came the Spring with all its splendor,
All its birds and all its blossoms,
All its flowers, and leaves, and grasses

—Longfellow

When the hounds Spring are on winter's traces,
The mother of months in meadow or plain
Fills the shadows and windy places
With lisp of leaves and ripple of rain.

—Swinburne

13

The Warm Embrace of Spring: A Time of New Possibilities

We grow great by dreams. All big men are dreamers.
They see things in the soft haze of a spring day,
Or in the fire on a long winter's evening.

Some of us let these great dreams die, but others
Nourish them and protect them through bad days,
Till they bring them to the sunshine and light…

Which comes always to those who sincerely
Hope that dreams will come true.

—Woodrow Wilson

One morning I was awakened by the sound of my next-door neighbor mowing his lawn. The sunlight pierced through the slightly closed blinds of my bedroom window. Slowly I got out of bed and walked over to the window. As I opened the blinds, the brilliant beams of sunlight scanned over my entire body. The warmth was like the embrace of my mother's loving arms. The yard was filled with a flourishing new coat of green, comprising thousands of blades of grass and hundreds of fresh blossoms. The trees and the flowers stretched forth their branches and stems toward the sky as if they, too, were being drawn into the arms of their loving Creator. He touched the womb of their fruitful existence with His arms of life. He spoke prosperity and growth into their seasonal process. The moment was filled with an ambiance of new possibilities, and I was there.

I'd always anticipated the spring season. For me, it was a time of new beginnings. Observing nature's blooming beauty seemed to impose its possibilities in my life. In many ways, it represented survival, more so, preservation while going through the refining fire of life. I have carried you on a journey with me through the seasons of refinement. If you're like me, whom I'm still in my state of becoming, you will concur with me that it has been, and still is, an eye-opening experience.

We've made it through the trial heat of summer, the cool pruning of fall, and the cold refinement of winter. Now we enter into the season that many await with baited breath, the season of spring. Nothing captures the true essence of the anticipation of new possibilities like the ambiance that accompanies the season of spring. Spring is definitely a time for blissful thinking. During this season, your mind will be open to clarity, creativity, and courageous and purposeful dreaming. You will no longer see yourself and the world through the previous tunnel vision. The dreamer in you that has longed to come forth can now take their rightful place in this world!

It is similar to the budding of a tree or the blooming of flowers at springtime. The ambiance is right … the environment has been prepared, and the vegetation of the earth cooperates with their destiny (God's timing to come forth and produce their fruit). So if you have come through the seasonal changes, the ambiance is conducive and the ground of your life is prepared for you to walk in line with or step into destiny and fulfill your purpose in life. Your potential gifts and talents are ready to emerge to assist you; all that is now needed is your awareness to the results of your renovated life. Take time to identify what changes have taken place in your thinking, your response to different situations, and how you coordinate your daily life as a whole. Now is the time to pay close attention to the details of your life. Because you are now planted in fertile soil, prosperity and divine promise will be yours. The burden of hopelessness has been replaced with success and personal fulfillment.

The bottom line is that you're starting a fresh. You are now presented with a new lease on life. Embrace it with all of your heart, soul, and spirit. Be careful not to instinctively backstroke into old patterns and methods of operations. Check yourself daily and intentionally. Make every decision with a new sense of purpose and clarity of thought based on your renewed mind. At first it may be mentally taxing, but eventually it will be like breathing air involuntarily, and you won't have to think twice about making decisions in the realm of truth. You have a built-in mechanism that will alert you to any possible problems or issues. The Spirit of God that dwells in you will guide you. During your seasons of refinement, you opened up your life to His direction and empowerment, so allow Him to advise you step-by-step for the remainder of your life's journey.

This is not about "spiritual spookyism." I'm referring to the innate impressions upon your heart, your mind, and your soul that can only come from the divine. You will unmistakably identify with what is a God idea, that is, the counsel of the infinite mind, versus your "old man" nature impulse. Because you are a refined person of purpose, anything that is not in line with truth will bring pause in your life and conflict in your heart. The choice, though obvious, will still be yours to make. Now that you have been cautioned, let's delve into some important aspects of your new beginning.

Take time to identify what changes have taken place in your thinking

A question came to mind as I prepared to write chapter 13 regarding the warm embrace of spring. The ambiance of possibilities is potent and all around you, but the question that is always asked and must be answered is: How do I bring these possibilities into my life or within my realm? You may ask whether this question has merit. Think with me for a moment. Has there been a time when you were in an environment with others who were elated and celebrating, but you could not connect with the excitement? Have you ever been in a setting that was ignited in celebration and noticed someone who looked like they didn't belong or seemed to have been on a date with the "Grinch Who Stole Christmas"? Well, that same scenario applies here. Possibilities are all around us, but there are some individuals who just can't get into the groove or into the flow. They fail to understand how to function in the season of possibilities.

Possibilities are attracted in the lives of individuals who possess and function in what I call the spirit of B.E.T. No, it is not the acronym for Black Entertainment Television. This one stands for *B*elief, *E*nthusiasm, *T*ake action. Anyone attempting to flow in spring's realm of possibilities is required to possess a personal belief that one is a candidate for possibilities. In other words, do not exempt yourself from anything God says is possible in your life. Move forward with an unshakeable spirit of expectation. Instead of dreading life, you should now embrace it. Your tears have been bottled up and have fermented throughout the passing seasons of life. In retrospect, you will drink from that vase of fermented affliction, for what was once a source of hurt is now transformed into wisdom and healing for your soul. Time processed your experience and brought illumination. Illumination exposed the lies of past failures and unlocked your possibilities. God, in His timing, has made everything beautiful and fruitful in your life. Concerning time, lies, and possibilities, William Shakespeare said, "Time's glory is to calm contending kings, to unmask falsehood, and bring truth to light." Your spring season is the fulfillment of that time in your life.

No more slow dancing to the blues of hopeless moments. You're now dancing the dance of freedom and singing the song of, "There is now no condemnation." Old things have passed away, and new things are on the horizon. I draw wisdom from Alfred Lord Tennyson who said, "The old order changeth, yielding place to the new ... and God fulfills Himself in many ways, lest one good custom should corrupt the world." You are to recognize your new place in life. Actualize your new freedom by embracing and pursuing your new possibilities with everything that is within you. You may stumble on the theory of worldly common sense when pursuing the possibilities of your destiny. A main deterrent to success in life is when someone says, "Use your common sense." This advice has the potential to halt your forward movement about something you passionately want to accomplish; some persons inject that to have you rethink your plans and/or actions according to old perceptions, which were probably shaped by them.

Check yourself daily and intentionally

The old maxim "Use your common sense," has its place if properly cultivated. I believe, however, that wisdom based on truth is more appropriate. Common sense is predicated on varied personal philosophies and depends on the *place* and *time* of its conception. Common sense, then, has the probability of being outdated and demographically irrelevant. Personally, I agree with Albert Einstein, a German-born theoretical physicist and the originator of the theory of relativity. He said, "Common sense is nothing more than a deposit of prejudices laid down in the mind before you reach eighteen." These are powerful words from one of the world's most esteemed individuals of his time.

Personal belief is an invaluable quality afforded to us as developing human beings. If not careful, it can be enslaved by the prejudices of common sense. The preconceived convictions and unfavorable conviction of others can be detrimental or injurious to a person who is hooked on the notion of common sense. Through focused personal belief, destiny will develop your sense of rationale; there will be nothing common about that experience. I believe that makes us all quite unique.

Belief

You must believe that you're a candidate for the realm of possibilities to engage your life. When the realm of possibility is engaged, we cross over the threshold of unbelief and enter into the realm of possibilities, where all things assigned to our destiny are possible, and the only limitations are those we place on ourselves. One of the most difficult concepts for many individuals to embrace is that their lives were decreed before they were even a passionate thought in their parents' minds. Your personal belief must begin with pondering this thought, "If God allowed my conception and birthing, then I am a part of His divine decree." He spoke these words to confirm this truth in the life of Jeremiah, whose name means, "Whom Jehovah has appointed." The divine decree revealed, "Before I formed you in the womb I knew you, before you were born I set you apart [decreed you]" (Jeremiah 1:5a NIV). Your possibilities are built in the divine decree of your life in the sphere of God's timing.

Your personal belief will be further strengthened when you understand the meaning of decree. Decree, by theological definition, is God's plan by means of which He has determined all things that relate to the universe, including His own actions toward it and everything that comes to pass in it and of it.[26] Therefore, by divine decree you have your existence because God determined a need for you in the world. In essence, you're here because of a void God saw in the earth that He determined only you could fill. So by divine decree, your purpose in life is predetermined, thus making it necessary for God to equip you with the potential to harness the possibilities that are already established and built into your purpose. So the season of spring in your life should be one of transcending limitations and moving into what I call the "possible impossibilities." Therefore, I say to you, whatever truth you've discovered about the why of your existence … it *is* attainable, and whatever the plan is for you in fulfilling your destiny … it *is* possible!

The following lines from an unknown author should challenge our belief and inspire us to move forward:

Child of My love, fear not the unknown morrow.
Dread not the new demand life makes of thee;
Thine ignorance doth hold no cause for sorrow,
For what thou knowest not is known to Me.

Thou canst not see today the hidden meaning
Of My command, but thou the light shall gain.
Walk on in faith, upon My promise leaning,
And as thou seest: Then go forward boldly;
One step is far enough for faith to see.
Take that, and thy next duty shall be told thee,
For step by step thy God is leading thee.

Stand not in fear, thine adversaries counting;
Dare every peril, save to disobey.
Thou shalt march on, each obstacle surmounting,
For I, the Strong, shall open up the way.
Therefore go gladly to the task assigned thee,
Having My promise; needing nothing more
Than just to know where'er the future find thee,
In all thy journeying—I GO BEFORE.

These verses should evoke a sense of anticipation and excitement about the next step in your journey. They speak volumes of God and how we should embrace, with personal and passionate belief, His promise of provision, protection, and completion of all possibilities apportioned to us.

Enthusiasm

An essential component of walking in the realm of springtime possibilities is enthusiasm. One definition for the word *enthusiasm* is the excited and passionate interest in, or eagerness to do something. It is an engrossing interest, something that arouses a consuming interest. Your springtime should be the object of your consuming interest. The many facets of your life that have been refined through the fires of summer; the pruned, separated, or detached debilitating issues dealt with in the fall of your life; and the purifying, meditative season of winter should have sparked a passion for new possibilities. We're born with a natural enthusiasm that can be eroded over time if we don't nourish and cultivate the seed. Like belief, enthusiasm is a quality that begins inside of us. It must be built into the full framework of the hope of those things that are made privy to us, those things that are at our grasp and are possible.

I remember well, in my late teens, how I perceived my future through the eyes of the dreamer inside me. There were so many plans, ideas, and goals I pondered each night before going to bed. They were the very thoughts I woke up to each morning that made living an anticipated and hopeful event. I had the whole world before me. In my heart and mind, I actually felt like there was nothing beyond my grasp. The span of time between my teens and early twenties seemed like one long spring season. Life was promising, and the success of my future seemed so tangible that I could almost touch and taste it. Then ... I grew up! Remember the common lies dealt with in previous chapters? I bought into and embraced those common lies that tend to cripple dreams. I fell captive to them. I began to question the validity of my dreams. My world was turned upside down, and the possibilities of my youth walked away from my youthful enthusiasm and fell into the adult, level-one, "think like everyone else" pessimism. As the years ensued, I began to notice that indeed, misery really does love company. I also discovered that the reason why I was being peer pressured, or should I say, subjected to friendships that obligated me into an emotional stupor, was because my enthusiasm toward life was shedding light on the uncertainties, misery, and mediocrity of many I trusted and thought were mutual dream sharers.

My challenge at hand was to find a way to recapture my God-given enthusiasm. It was a gift that I allowed others to steal away from me. The process, I later found out, was exactly what we've just come through in the reading of this text. Once I made it through the deprogramming stages and began renewing my thought-life, I experienced the resurrection of my youthful enthusiasms. Once again, the possibilities of my life reemerged. Since then, I've neither looked back nor *listened* back! The impairing voices of my past no longer had any effect on my enthusiasm. This is where you need to be at this point in your life, a proper mind-set renovated through the seasonal adjustments. This God-given gift of enthusiasm belongs to you as well. It is a treasure that should not be hidden but exposed. It should never be extinguished, but experienced; and this experience should be shared with everyone whose life intersects yours.

Your life should now be taking the shape of destiny's unique pattern, a pattern meticulously planned and purposed specifically to fit you. Use your enthusiasm to fuel movement toward your purpose. By virtue of its definition, enthusiasm is an eagerness to do something. I see enthusiasm built in a statement made by a self-made merchant, John Wanamaker, who said, "A man is not doing much until the cause he works for possesses all there is of him." Enthusiasm, when nurtured, is desire. Desire, when harnessed, is power.

Failure to nurture enthusiasm and harness desire, and failure to act on what your destiny requires you to accomplish or become, paves the way to mediocrity. The attitude of enthusiasm does make a difference. Professor Erwin H. Schell, a much-respected authority on leadership, says, "Obviously, there is something more than facilities and competence that makes for accomplishment.

I have come to believe that this linkage factor, this catalyst, if you will, can be defined in a single word—*attitude*. When our attitude is right, our abilities reach a maximum of effectiveness, and good results inevitably follow."[27] Develop your attitude of enthusiasm, for when you do, you will experience a deep, burning desire that will make your commitment to purpose a love affair with destiny.

Take Action

Your love affair with destiny will not allow you to be idle and watch life pass you by. It will stir up something within you that will require you to act upon your reason for life. Our latent abilities need a stimulant to release the potential that is stored up within. That stimulant is responsibility. You have a responsibility on your shoulders to initiate the plan for your life's purpose. You are the only one responsible for the fulfillment of your destiny. You now have to take that step of faith into the arena of life reserved especially for your participation. You've been given access to the treasures of destiny concerning why you are and who you are. The Bible states that, "To whom much is given, much is required" (Luke 12:48). Are you willing to pay the price?

Responsibility is a fair price to pay for the new possibilities that have availed themselves to you as a result of you taking action and taking charge of your life. According to our twenty-sixth president of the United States, Theodore Roosevelt, "Your ability needs responsibility to expose its possibilities." By extension, he said, "Do what you can with what you have where you are." What a profound and stimulating statement. So how does responsibility tie in with taking action? Responsibility is not only a rhetorical and theoretical position; it denotes the ability to *respond* to life's situations and tap into its reserved possibilities.

I use the term "reserved" because there is untapped potential and unlimited possibilities reserved for you. These will not be exposed or made available to you until something happens to trigger your awareness of their existence. Case in point: I was a youth, fourteen years old, thinking of the next adventure to explore in my young life. In our front yard, there was a wooden fence my father built; it was the entrance to our yard. Directly in front of the wooden fence, there stood a beautiful, tall tree with many branches extending from it. Springtime had settled in, and the acorns that adorned this tree were already visible. The lowest branch was about twice my height at that time. I'd been contemplating trying to jump the height necessary to reach the branch so that I could climb up into the tree and survey the neighborhood. I had never done it before, and the few guys in the neighborhood who had attempted it previously were unsuccessful, so I gave up the hope of ever accomplishing my goal of climbing that tree.

One day I was riding my bike around the block, which was a daily ritual. Something was about to occur that would change my perception and my life. At top speed, I approached our neighbor's house, which was located directly behind ours. The reason for this is that they had a dog named Trixie. Now Trixie, I believed, was mixed German shepherd and Fox terrier. She was an intimidating animal to be reckoned with. As long as I was on my bike at top speed, I was fine. I kind of got a kick from outrunning her on my bike; the experience made me a young champion of sorts. Well this particular day, according to my riding ritual, I built up my speed as I approached the challenging perimeter of my neighbor's yard. Like clockwork, Trixie was waiting and soon took off behind me. Normally, the chase would only last a fourth of a block and then Trixie would give up and return home. This day would prove to be different.

Our latent abilities need a stimulant to release the potential that is stored up within

As I approached Trixie's "give up" distance, something happened that had never happened before: my chain broke!

My peddling capabilities were incapacitated (to say the least). By now, Trixie's instincts alerted her that this was a once-in-a-lifetime opportunity to make up for all her past defeats. By this time, my heart was racing, my head was throbbing, and fear quickly overshadowed me as I had already envisioned Trixie biting me, sending shock waves of pain throughout my entire body. Operating in sheer survival mode, I threw my bike on the ground and began running around the corner of the block where our house was located. I could feel Trixie's warm breath around my ankles. Her barking, mixed with an antagonizing growl, heightened my need to avoid getting caught and devoured.

As soon as I approached my front yard, my first impulse was to climb the fence, but I knew if I did, because Trixie was so close behind me, she would conquer me. Without thinking or rationalizing the challenge, I jumped straight up, and I felt my fingers wrap around the branch of the tree I had long wanted to climb, and I pulled myself up into the tree. Unaware of what I had achieved, I sat on the branch of that tree with my arms wrapped tightly around its trunk. Needless to say, I was in sheer horror. I reluctantly glanced down to assess my situation only to witness Trixie leaping back and forth in anger … barking and growling because of her missed opportunity.

A few minutes passed, and a defeated Trixie settled down and returned home. It was at that moment that I realized what I had unknowingly and unintentionally done. The challenge that presented itself in my situation proved to be what was needed to expose my hidden potential and nurture my future possibilities of achieving whatever is in my destiny. Trixie placed the responsibility of escaping peril on my abilities, which in turn exposed my potential. In essence, you've got to take action to move and flow in the new possibilities the spring season of your life has presented. Even if it means taking one step at a time, act, attempt, and move toward the changes you want in your life, or the hope you've dreamed about. The method for transitioning from the old you to your renewed perception of yourself, and the creative ideas that now fill your fertile mind toward action, can be summed up in one of the most effective slogans I've seen in commercial advertising. In the Nike footwear commercial, these three words drive home a valuable concept: "Just do it!"

Rest in the arms of spring's warm embrace; enjoy the ambiance of the new possibilities available to you now. Don't spend time worrying about weaknesses and shortcomings. God is still working on those variables in your life; you're a *being* in process. So never use weaknesses and shortcomings as an excuse for the stagnation in your life. As you move forward, you will work through your weaknesses and shortcomings. Remember, you're evolving into the "who" you're to be; it will take a lifetime. Resolve to be proactive; don't wait until conditions are perfect, as they never will be. You should expect difficulties and obstacles as you move toward your destiny; resolve them as they arise, but make sure you keep moving. You will discover that as you keep moving toward your destiny, you will overcome one obstacle after another. Eventually, because you take action constantly in the face of life's many challenges, fear will transition from a stagnating hindrance, to a fuel—propelling you toward achieving your purpose.

Finally, begin to think in terms of "now." *Tomorrow, next week, later,* and similar words often are synonymous with the failure word "never." In the words of the late president John F. Kennedy, "Never put off till tomorrow what you can do today." Take action now, dig in, and move forward toward your new possibilities. "Just do it!" Here is a gem I learned from childhood:

> Putting off till tomorrow
> Will lead us to sorrow
> Beginning today
> Is the very best way.

14

A Time of Exposing Your Inner Beauty: The New and Improved You

When old age this generation waste,
Thou shalt remain, in midst of other woe
Than ours, a friend to man, to whom thou say'st,
"Beauty is truth, truth beauty,"—that is all
Ye know on earth, and all ye need to know.

—John Keats

Beauty has different definitions depending on the venue of interpretation to which you subscribe. Aesthetics is a branch of philosophy concerned with the essence and perception of beauty and ugliness. Aesthetics also deals with the question of whether such qualities are objectively present in the things they appear to qualify, or if they exist only in the mind of the individual; hence, the argument is whether objects are perceived by a particular mode, the aesthetic mode, or instead have, in themselves, special qualities—aesthetic qualities. Philosophy also asks if there is a difference between the beautiful and the sublime. An overwhelming majority of society subscribe to the notion that beauty is relatively an exterior quality. In the temporal world of delusion, this is a truism, but in the deeper world of spirituality, it is not the truth. Have you ever experienced meeting a physically beautiful individual and, after spending time with them, you find that they possess a despicable personality and disposition? It literally changes your perception of that individual; the inner quality taints the exterior quality, and he or she suddenly becomes unattractive as a personal being.

Please don't misunderstand my implication; I appreciate external beauty like anybody else. My approach to this subject is not an attempt to disqualify or dismiss the appeal of external beauty but to turn your attention to the most neglected, yet most vital beauty accessible to all of humanity who sincerely searches for it. Inner beauty, birthed through the illumination of "truth," is a most significant element of personal assurance and empowerment given to mankind. According to the temporal delusion of world opinion, external beauty is afforded to whom they deem deserving of such accolades based on very biased, superficial, and limited exterior qualifiers.

Society's expectation to cultivate and maintain exterior beauty serves as a lethal contemporary weapon to occupy the minds of both men and women today. If you're preoccupied with the exterior self, more than likely, something else is being neglected: the true *you*. The true you is the person of the heart and the "being" of the soul. Because exterior beauty and social expectations require so much time, money, and emotional effort, you're left with no energy or interest in nurturing and developing spiritually. Remember, we're not only body; we are body, soul, and spirit beings. I guess the perception of many is that the approval and acceptance of others is more important than personal acceptance and divine approval.

If this is true, your self-image and your personal significance are directly proportioned to your exterior beauty and societal acceptance. Should this be the case, please note that as time passes and beauty fades, so fades your self-image and your personal significance. On the other hand, if your self-image and significance are in direct proportion with God and His unchanging truth about you and your life's inner beauty, then you're able to maintain a fulfilled personal life, a healthy self-image, and a powerful sense of significance that will be consistent throughout life's changing times, regardless of how much your physical features change.

Poetry is an important and satisfying part of my life. There are many poets whose pieces I enjoy reading, and John Keats is among my favorites. At the very beginning of this chapter is a verse from one of his poems. It relates significantly to the discussion of paralleling nature with humanity, beauty with truth. John Keats (1795–1821) was a major English poet. Despite his early death from tuberculosis at the age of twenty-five, Keats's poetry describes the beauty of the natural world and art as the vehicle for his poetic imagination. His career was brief, but we see his poetry evolve from this love of nature and art into a deep compassion for humanity. The final lines of Keats's "Ode on a Grecian Urn" were written when he was twenty-three years old. He found the highest form of meaning in *pure* beauty. According to the compassionate poet, the urn is unchanged through the centuries, and that moment of eternal beauty is frozen in time. One should look beyond the moment since it does not bring us any gain.[28]

Keats's poetic piece raises a vital question: "What is most important in life?" We spend so much time, energy, and emotions on things in life that have momentary value and social significance. I'm not in any way suggesting that these must be totally neglected, but as *personal beings*, whose primary interest should be evolving innately into our best selves, discovering what is true about our human and spiritual nature should be priority. Our human or natural dimension is temporary; it fades like a momentary experience with water's vapor. Our spiritual nature is eternal, like the beauty of the urn in Keats's poem; it lasts through time, and in this scenario … even beyond time. Understanding what aspects of our being are eternal should assist us in appropriately determining where to invest our time, energy, emotions, and resources. As I study people and their behaviors, it is apparent that more attention is given to the temporary physical dimension than the spiritual dimension, which will transcend into a timeless existence. It is imperative that there be a shift in the paradigm of our priorities.

The true you is the person of the heart, and the "being" of the soul

Keats shares the Bible's use of parallels with humanity, nature, and animation to illuminate relevant, eternal principles that expand our understanding of a particular subject matter. He utilized poetry to magnify the beauty of the natural world and art as the vehicle for his poetic imagination. The writer of the book of Philippians also utilized the following inspired biblical writing to illustrate humanity's source of origin and beauty, "For we are God's workmanship" (Philippians 2:10*a*). The Greek word for workmanship is *poyema,* from which the English word *poem* or *poetry* is derived. In essence, the writer is saying that, "We are God's poetry." Our origin and existence are to be the very expression of God's beauty and love on the earth. Why are we God's beauty? Keats said, "Beauty is truth, truth beauty." I refer to truth as the divine eternal truth, decreed by the omniscient God. Our best and perfected "self" is found in that divine decree. But as beings in our state of *becoming*, we are God's "work in progress." During the journey of life, our relationship with Him exposes a beauty within us that time can never erase, and a beauty that will echo into eternity.

Returning to the parallel of nature and humanity, nothing is more spectacular than to witness the birthing, or coming forth, of the hidden beauty of nature at springtime. What was once tucked away under the ground, on the limb, or in the stem now protrudes with new life from its source of being. Having submitted to the processes of summer's heat, fall's pruning, and winter's purification, time sanctions the release of its beauty. We who have submitted to the processes of the seasonal changes in life can't help experiencing our predetermined, time-released inner beauty. This principle is confirmed in the ancient writing of a biblical poet and king. According to Solomon, king of Israel, "There is a time for everything, and a season for every activity under heaven.... I have seen the burden God has laid on men.... He has made everything beautiful in its time" (Ecclesiastes 3:1, 10, 11 NIV).

Our beauty complements the beauty of nature, yet it transcends what is visible into that which impacts the soul and spirit of humanity. The outward beauty of nature captures the eye and brings pause to the heart of man. The innate beauty of renewed mankind does even more; it brings pause and also gives the soul of man reason for living. Our inner beauty helps to sharpen the awareness of other individuals' *cause* for being. We become a reflection of God's possibilities in their lives.

There are many identifying qualities of inner beauty, but permit me to identify what I feel are the foundational qualities from which the rest originate: a renewed knowledgeable spirit life, a healthy self-esteem under the accountability of humility, a contagious enthusiasm toward life, an abounding unconditional love, and a visionary.

A Renewed Knowledgeable Spirit Life

We spoke about the importance and process of a renewed spiritual life in previous chapters. The key word in this particular quality is *knowledge*. Our old nature, or self, operated in ignorance in relation to very important facets of the spiritual life. Your inner beauty will reflect a deeper "knowing" concerning life and how you fit. Ignorance is the most powerful tool of the old man's nature. The Webster's Dictionary defines ignorance as the "quality or condition of little knowledge, education or experience"; it is an unawareness. When we use ignorance to describe our understanding of our true selves and where we fit in the scheme of purpose, it means that we have little knowledge, education, or experience concerning the reason for our existence. It means we are blindsided to the divine decree of God concerning our being. We are unaware of His plans and purposes for our lives, and our existence becomes a trial-and-error game.

Ignorance of this nature tarnishes our innate spiritual beauty. It is threatening, because it permits us to think that there is the possibility that we will live out our lives not knowing who we are or why we live. Such thinking is a dark cloud that cloaks the inner beauty. But if you've come through the seasons that are necessary for change, and you have made it to the springtime of your life's experiences, you are no longer tarnished with a deficit of knowledge. Knowing of the who and why of your existence should saturate your very being, enhancing the ambiance of your inner beauty. Such an ambiance emits a sphere of confidence that moves through you, around you, and from you. Everyone who comes in contact with you will experience your innate beauty in one way or another. Your newfound beauty will touch the core of other individuals and prompt them to rethink the who and why of their existence.

Your renewed knowledgeable spirit life is a lasting quality of inner beauty. It will outlive the body that houses the real you. The maintenance of this quality of innate beauty requires a continual connectedness with God, the source of life. Our responsibility to this unfading inner beauty is that we continue to nurture it through prayer and meditation and reading the Bible and other inspirational and empowering literature that are truth-oriented materials. We are responsible for connecting with other dream sharers who are committed to the maturation and personal growth process. The exciting element about this quality is that as time passes, unlike physical beauty, with proper nurturing, the inner beauty increases and is magnified to greater dimensions of exposure. In other words, your inner beauty will be impossible to hide or ignored if you're properly attending to its details.

Jesus Christ described the undeniable innate beauty of

renewed mankind this way: "You are the light of the world. A city on a hill cannot be hidden … let your light shine before men" (Matthew 5:14, 16*b* NIV). Likewise, King Solomon gives us a splendid, poetic view of the radiant walk and inner beauty of a spiritually changed individual when he said, "The path of the righteous is like the first gleam of dawn, shining ever brighter till the full light of day" (Proverbs 4:18 NIV).

A Healthy Self-Esteem Under the Accountability of Humility

A renewed knowledgeable spirit life will give birth to another quality of inner beauty, a healthy self-esteem under the accountability of humility. A healthy self-esteem is when an individual operates in a spirit of confidence. Not confidence that is overwhelming and matriculates into a spirit of pride, but one that is checked by humility. Your past experiences, especially through the summer/trial season and the fall/pruning season, should have brought pause to your life and an understanding that your life is under a divine mandate. As such, your life is dependent on God, the infinite source, to achieve any and all things predetermined as your purpose and destiny in life. Our confidence has its life in that divine arrangement. If we walk outside of this arrangement or covenant, we are alienated from divine assistance, hence, subjecting ourselves to more corrective trials, errors, and failures, which in turn affect our confidence level.

But since we, who have come through the seasons that are necessary for change, know that we have our being and existence in Him who has given us life, our confidence is secure in the humility birthed during our trial and pruning process. There has always been something attractive about an individual who oozes with confidence. It doesn't matter what that person's exterior quality may or may not be; if the innate quality of confidence is present, it will shine forth from the individual. A biblical writer admonishes us, "So do not throw away your confidence; it will be richly rewarded. You need to persevere so that when you have done the will of God, you will receive what He has promised" (Hebrews 10:35–36 NIV). I use confidence and self-esteem synonymously because both are closely related. They originate from and depend on their source. In no way do I imply exclusive self-reliance; I totally embrace the fact that we are cooperative vessels moving with the rhythm of the Spirit of God, flowing through us and around us, fulfilling all predetermined goals in life. With that in mind, we are totally confident of the guaranteed success in all that He predetermines and performs through us. Such confidence produces a contagious enthusiasm toward life.

A Contagious Enthusiasm Toward Life

Enthusiasm is an inner, electrifying persona that sparks and sets fire to whatever and whomever it comes in contact with. Enthusiasm is the product of successful experiences used to build confidence, which in turn stimulates the anticipation of the successes of future challenges. Enthusiasm flows from this reflection of past successes into your present situations in life. As you will soon find out, enthusiasm is a key element in motivating others to embrace you and your dreams. It will motivate others to invest valuable resources in your pursuit of purpose. Take note: in order to activate others, to get them to be enthusiastic, you must first be enthusiastic; you must first set yourself on fire with enthusiasm. As your life is intersected with the individuals predetermined to be a part of your experiences in life, they will be positively impacted by this quality of innate beauty.

Confidence and enthusiasm breathe life into a lifeless relationship and/or experience. Think for a moment about relationships, meetings, conferences, and organizations that lack enthusiasm. How do you feel when you're directly involved in such lifeless situations? Exactly! You're bored, drained, and feel a nagging sense of wasted time. In many cases, this is the prevailing attitude concerning life, and it seems as if life is just fading away all around you; that is, until you come in contact with someone who has been reenergized. Their inner beauty and quality of enthusiasm touches you and breathes life back into your lifeless existence. It has been said that the results in life come in direct proportion to the enthusiasm applied. So the refined you must exhibit this quality in every aspect of your life until it becomes a permanent part of your nature and everyday mode of operation. Then prepare yourself for the results that are destined to follow. Make no mistake, you'll love the results!

Like any new quality you now possess, it will require development. An important aspect of developing enthusiasm is learning more about the person, organization, situation, or thing you are not enthusiastic about. "Knowledge is power," even as it relates to enthusiasm. I intentionally explore a situation I cannot identify with. My reason is to discover an aspect of the situation that can be the motivating factor that will assist me to embrace it as a meaningful experience. I'm frequently approached and questioned as to whether I smile all the time. People ask me this question ever so often because no matter where I am or what situation I'm involved in, I bring my inner beauty into the mix. I see every human encounter as an opportunity to extend my inner beauty. My inner beauty—what is it? Well, in the most preliminary and basic explanation, it is a warm smile birthed from a genuine universal love for humanity. It is a confident greeting and a brief, enthusiastic dialogue. There is so much more that can be added to the list, but those three, I feel, are critical. I have turned some most unfortunate circumstances around because I chose to "life up" a seemingly routine encounter with enthusiasm. You can do that, too!

Seize every opportunity to expose this empowering quality to the world. When you're with family, friends, or career associates, find something fascinating to share with them. Focus on amusing, empowering, and life-giving conversations. Let the unpleasant things stay at bay until you're able to share it with a close, credible confidante and come to a resolution. It has been my experience that engaging in irresolvable debate is pointless. It only incites worry, exaggerates improbable outcomes, and nurtures fear. There is an overabundance of complainers (doom-and-gloom prognosticators) in the world. Dare to be different; bring some beauty in the midst of a traumatized world. The reality is that people need motivation, and they love to be around lively, enthusiastic people.

An Abounding Unconditional Love

Unconditional love defies the thought that, "Those who fail in life are unworthy of love and deserve to be punished." Have you ever wondered how a critical or judgmental person lives with himself or herself? The answer—not very well. If we perceive success or failure as our primary source of evaluating ourselves and others, or if we believe performance reflects one's value and that failure makes one unacceptable and unworthy of love, then we usually feel completely justified in condemning those who fail, as well as ourselves. Self-depreciation and self-condemnation are enemies to your ability to exhibit love. The Bible instructs us to, "Love one another as we love ourselves." The qualifying prerequisite for expressing true love is found in that verse of Scripture; it is found in knowing how to first love your *self.* Relational abuse can be traced back to the abuser's lack or inability to accept and truly love himself for whatever reason(s). The spring season exposes the "love work" of the previous seasons. The individual displays a fond appreciation for their personal life and the lives of others.

In writing to the Philippians, Paul said, "And this is my prayer: that your love may abound more and more in knowledge and depth of insight" (Philippians 1:9 NIV). This is the foundational quality of inner beauty that should be the prevailing emphasis of all that we are and will ever be. It is also the fuel of purpose and the driving force behind our destiny. True love is nondiscriminating; it defies all logic and resides in a realm beyond natural understanding. This foundational quality of inner beauty invites all to experience its warm acceptance and comforting embrace. To bring clarity and a deeper understanding of the love we're to exhibit, we must first explore the basic tenet of the love exemplified by God, our source. The love of God and His acceptance of us are based on a powerful concept or tenet we've come to know as *grace*, His unmerited favor. This is a very important aspect of the inner beauty quality of love. This aspect of love is important simply because it is not based on our ability, or the ability of others, to impress the other through good deeds or behavior.

This is a spiritually oriented kind of love that transcends beyond our *emotional* love and directs us to *volitional* love. Spiritual love is *agape* love, which means to love in a moral sense; it is a deliberate act of the will as a matter of principle, duty, and propriety. The new you understands that the heart, the inner self, is comprised of three parts: the *intellect* (soul) being the *rational you*, the *will* (spirit) the *volitional you*, and the *feelings* (body) the *emotional you*. You are to love others volitionally, as an act of the will by choice. Fortunately, you are not required to *feel* in love with others. Contrary to the song that made it to the top of the charts, you may or may not get that "loving feeling." But the love that we're to focus on is a decision made as a deliberate act of the will. Your feelings may be affected in one way or another, but spiritual love is a decision, not a feeling. This is how you will be able to express unconditional love. It is initially a conscious act that eventually manifests into tangible expressions of that love.

God's amazing grace compels us to action, because love motivates us to please the One who has freely loved us. As others experience our unconditional love, they will be motivated to respond by reciprocating an expression of their love to us. It may not be as quickly or in the same manner as we've expressed it, but the attempt or response will be a positive reflection of what they've experienced from us. Therefore, we must seek to explore and expose the potential love in everyone we meet, allowing them to experience the essence of God in themselves as well as in us. Let love have her perfect work in your life. A truly renewed and changed individual will move beyond the prognostic and rhetorical expression of love and begin to provide displayed works of love through unconditional acceptance, genuine forgiveness, nonjudgmental attitude, encouragement, and heartfelt benevolence.

A Visionary

Michelangelo is a perfect example of a visionary. The story is told of a visitor who interrupted him in his studio and asked, "What are you doing?" At that time, the great artist had just received a magnificent piece of marble. He began at once to chisel one of the corners, working at what appeared to be a wing. Listen to his answer to the visitor: "There is an angel imprisoned within the marble, and I am trying to set him free." Within the marble was a vision that Michelangelo was bringing into fruition. Like Michelangelo, locked inside the heart of every individual is a visionary with only the tip of its wing showing. Spring exposes, piece by piece, who the visionary is and what the visionary sees. It exposes that innate quality of the special sight we call ... *vision*.

Vision does not only mean *see*, it also means to *come into being*. The Webster's Dictionary defines vision as, "the ability to perceive something not actually visible, as through mental acuteness or keen foresight." To appropriate these meanings and apply them to the inner beauty quality that you are to expose now, it is reasonable to say that a visionary is one who looks not at what is at the present but at what could or should be. The defining value of purpose is the translation of vision derived from purpose and propels into a plan of action; it brings precision to life. One writer said, "If you don't know where you are going in life, how will you know when you get there?" Purpose provides the resolve to that question, because it involves a vision, which in turn, motivates a plan of action to meet specific goals in life.

There is something extraordinary about individuals who not only know who they are but also where they are going in life. Without question, as soon as you come into contact with them, you immediately sense that they transcend the waste of abstract living, the misdirection of the unfocused, and the unprofitibility of the procrastinator. They are the movers and shakers of this world. As a visionary, you are a mover and a shaker. Your will becomes consumed with accomplishing that which is in your heart and mind that burns daily in the realm of destiny. Your budding passions for this life spring forth and reveal themselves. Like an acorn or a rose in the prelude of spring, your vision is a glimpse of that which is about to come into fruition. It is a guiding light that will shine through you into a cloudy world, exposing yet another dimension of the new refined you that can only be described as ... beautiful!

The world is beautiful because they (visionary) have lived;
Without them, laboring humanity would perish ...
He who cherishes a beautiful vision, a lofty ideal in his heart,
Will one day realize it. Columbus cherished a vision of
Another world, and he discovered it ...

Cherish your visions; cherish your ideals; cherish the music
That stirs in your heart, the beauty that forms in your mind,
The loveliness that drapes your purest thoughts, for out of
Them will grow all delightful conditions, all heavenly
Environment; of these, if you but remain true to them,
Your world will at last be built.

—James Allen

15

X-Ray Your Vision: Examining and Pursuing Your Future Goals in Life

Write down the vision and make it plain on tablets
so that a herald may run with it. For the vision
awaits an appointed time; it speaks of the end
and will not prove false. Though it linger,
wait for it; it will certainly come
and will not delay.

—Habakkuk 2:2–3 (paraphrased)

In chapter 14, we discovered that vision is not only the ability to *see*, but it is also to ignite action for the innately realized path, to *come into being*. In this chapter, we are going to take a closer look at some of the essentials necessary in future goal setting and planning to bring to fruition … your vision. I deliberately chose to include "x-ray" in the chapter title so as to emphasize the meticulous care that should be taken as you work on goal setting and planning. To understand how critical x-raying your vision is, to success in life, let's take a brief look at how X-rays are used. X-ray is the abbreviated term for electromagnetic radiation. An X-ray is a relatively high-energy photo with a wavelength stream used for its penetrating power to magnify an object through existing material. Physicians use X-rays to penetrate the body's flesh to get a picture of what can't be seen with the naked eye. In essence, X-rays penetrate the exterior to view the interior, the vital organs that keep human beings alive and functioning.

Growing up as a kid, I had many fascinations. One of them was with the extraordinary power of my favorite superhero, Superman. Among his many superhuman attributes was the ability to see through steel with his X-ray vision. I always marveled at this ability, because Superman was able to stay abreast of potential dangers and pitfalls. We need to embrace the concept of X-ray vision and utilize it to scrutinize the vision of our past. This kind of penetrating power is needed for the visionary in you. It is the ability to see through and beyond the crusted remains of your old expectations, goals, and plans. It magnifies the vital organs of destiny (purpose and vision), exposing what cannot be seen with the eyes of the past.

During your spring season, it will be a time of analyzing and refocusing vision. What has worked, or not worked, for you in the yesteryears of your life are no longer appropriate for the new you. Attempting to flow and function as a renewed person in old methods and crisis-driven goals is like trying to operate a Jaguar with a Ford Pinto engine.

You're much wiser and larger than that now! The *old self* (the old you) was a person whose motivation for living was self-centered, whose outlook on life was negatively habitual. The old you would look at life from the perspective of finite self. The mind-set of that individual of the past was that their whole orientation is to think, act, and feel as you always have; that is, accepting your imposed limitations and questionable future outlook. The seasons you've come through were a process that assisted you in allowing this habitual mind-set and way of life to die in favor of the new life you've been given. The dimensions of your personhood have transcended the limitations of the past. You've outsourced the small vision of the past that based its outlook on imposed debilitating factors. You have the infinite source abiding within your renewed being, waiting to release His potential in you to fulfill the expanded dimensions of your vision and everything involved in accomplishing His ultimate destiny in your life.

The above affirmation of promise alone is enough to ignite anyone and set them in flight in pursuit of fulfilling their destiny. As motivated as you may be at this point, because of your new lease on life, there are some preliminary details to attend to before rushing into doing what you think is a good idea. It has been said that, "Good ideas are not necessarily God ideas." So as an initial priority, you should begin the process of examining your goals and plan prudently according to your new heart's desires.

Vision must be followed by the venture. What a powerful statement of truth! But an individual must x-ray their vision for clarity and understanding before proceeding to venture. As quoted in chapter 14, "If you don't know where you are going in life, how will you know when you get there?" Destiny is the predetermined point, or points, in life that you are to arrive at and the functions in life you are to achieve. I believe that life consists of many intermediate destinies, whose sum total represents our ultimate destiny. It is similar to taking a trip from south Florida to north Florida. Ponder this concept. If I desire to take a trip from West Palm Beach to Jacksonville, although my destination is Jacksonville, there are many cities, exits, and highways that must be reached (intermediate destinies) to arrive at my final destination. If you've never taken that trip before, then you will need a road map to plan your trip. Vision is life's road map; it reveals the routes toward destiny. Vision is where we begin to plan and set goals for our trip in life; without it we perish. An old adage gives a contemporary interpretation, "Those who fail to plan, plan to fail."

These plans must be based on authentic vision that is birthed in the mind of God and shared with you for its implementation on earth. His thoughts concerning His plans and purpose in your life are confirmed in your heart and soul. It is something that should never be guessed or assumed. A major aspect in x-raying your vision is to determine its origin. A vision produced without the benefit of consulting God's decreed plan is subject to failure and finite limitations. A vision birthed according to the decree (will) of God is promised success, unlimited support, provisions, and protection.

I have been counseling with individuals on a yearly basis, and I'm amazed at the many that come to me brokenhearted, depressed, and discouraged about life because things just aren't working out for them. Every year they face similar trials, disappointments, and end-of-year results. When I ask them about their goals and plans, their response is, "I'm not doing anything differently from how I've always done them," as if that was really something to brag about. My usual response to that statement is, "That is exactly why things are not progressing for you!"

The vision must be followed by the venture

Individuals like these may have come up with a concept for success or some advice that may have worked to some degree for other persons. Here is the problem: they tried to appropriate the same principle in their lives only to find that the advice or principle is archaic, or maybe it is just a principle that is totally irrelevant to their situation. Rather than changing methods and searching for a better way, they just keep applying the methods and principles that have proven ineffective. I guess they are hoping that in some odd mystical moment they will experience a breakthrough.

What I generally do is formulate with them a definition for insanity: insanity is doing the same things over and over again expecting different results. The problem arises when we embrace a vision or method of operation that worked at one point or another for us or someone we know who passed it on to us, and we attempt to perpetuate it. I believe that each year we need to rethink our goals and plans to ensure we're still on track with vision. It is possible to miss an exit or make a wrong turn on a trip. Likewise, it is possible to get off course while on your journey in life. So to assist you, we shall take a look at four important factors in vision planning and goal setting.

Factor 1: View Your Vision Through the Corrective Lens of Truth

X-raying your vision allows you to see through the layers of life's imposed obstructions. An X-ray in this instance is an initial "eye-opening" jolt to expose you to what belongs to you, and it represents your life's aspirations. To continue seeing your future properly, you must adjust your everyday "special sight" (vision) with the corrective lens of truth. Let's look at it in this respect. When there is a problem with one's physical ability to see, it is normal for one to make an appointment to see an optometrist. At that point, various tests are performed to ascertain the cause of the problem, the extent of the problem, and determine the strength of the corrective lens to be prescribed.

Likewise, during the previous seasons, we submitted to the various tests of the divine optometrist, and those tests revealed some interesting debilitating issues that blurred our vision. We've come through the seasonal tests and have made it to the season of beauty, the season of spring. Spring is, among many other wonderful descriptions, a time of clear skies. As a poet, I sometimes use this metaphor, "the mind's clear sky" to evoke imagery to a poetic piece that depicts the awareness of an individual coming into a mental place of realization. Truth has a way of magnifying, clearing, and bringing a sense of realization into any situation. Vision is corrected by such realizations. Each day that we awake, we should be cognizant of which visionary lens we're using to view our path. Fatalists do not care about such a concept; they accept whatever they see through whatever lens they are presented at the wake of each morning.

You are not a fatalist; you are a visionary. You are not moved by what you initially see each morning. You are aware that there is a possibility that the old thought-life that once possessed your thinking is capable of reflecting illusions of the past that will lure you off course. You understand that your life's course has been predetermined and set. The only thing required is that you see your life's course through the lens of destiny and flow toward the expected results based on truth. It has been said that "Your vision is the promise of what you shall one day be; your ideal is the prophecy of what you shall at last unveil." When the X-ray of vision reveals that which was previously unseen, you will develop a passion that will grip the heart and soul of everything that represents all of who you are. It will give life to your motivation and finishing grace to your pursuit.

Factor 2: Understanding and Recording the Vision

(a) Understanding the Vision

It is one thing to see something and quite another to understand what you see. The proverbial affirmation firmly states that, "Wisdom is supreme; therefore get wisdom. Though it cost all you have, get understanding" (Proverbs 4:7 NIV). Wisdom (the ability to make use of knowledge effectively) is described as supreme in this verse, but understanding (clarity of knowledge, the ability to discern and organize thoughts for its true meaning) is the jewel of all "learning." The writer of this proverb continues to express the importance of understanding by saying, "Wisdom rests in the heart of him that hath understanding" (Proverbs 14:33*a*), and "Understanding is a fountain of life to those that have it, but folly brings punishment to fools" (Proverbs 16:22 NIV). There is a reason for such grave insistence and high moral value in getting understanding. If you fail to get understanding of an idea or a principle, it will be as if you were never exposed to that idea or principle. If this happens, you will continue to operate in error and reap the meager rewards of ignorance.

Misinterpreted vision is as lethal as having no vision at all. This can be likened to the importance of a map in reaching a particular destination. If you have a map but do not understand how to properly interpret the information, the probability of you reaching your predetermined goal or destination will be bleak! *Understanding* reduces error, redeems or saves time, and increases goal efficiency. Pursuing destiny and fulfilling vision is not exempted from this important element of life called *understanding.* It is dangerous to have foresight (vision) but have no insight (understanding). To live life in such a manner proves to be waste of time and an endless list of things to do without the benefit of a sense of fulfillment. The apostle Paul, a brilliant mind of his time, sums up this concept when he says,

> Therefore I do not run like a man running aimlessly;
> I do not fight like a man beating the air.
> (1 Corinthians 9:26)

(b) Recording the Vision

I have read many books on personal empowerment and development, but none compares to the offerings of biblical concepts. In fact, almost all of the secular empowerment literatures I've read are laced with biblical principles as the foundation from which authors build their ideas or suppositions; of course they put their own spin to it. So if you want infallible truth, go directly to the source. As it pertains to vision, the Bible admonishes us to write down our visions and make them plain (Habakkuk 2:2). Writing things down make them real to the mind, which is nurtured by perception. For every goal in life there must be a written plan.

Recording your plans burns them into the mental complex

(conscious, subconscious, and conscience) for long-term memory, future retrieval, and application. When recording your plan of action concerning vision, you are systematically scheduling events and directives that will yield measurable results. When God gives you a vision, He always shows you enough to form a plan in which you should have some idea of the expected results. Otherwise, you will not know whether you're achieving your goals toward fulfilling vision.

Recording your vision is the most effective tool that enables you to mentally visualize and internalize your plans, which in turn helps to crystallize the vision and its desired end result. I am an advocate of keeping a personal journal; it is a source of visualization and internalization. I personally have kept one for many years, recording my thoughts, dreams, and insights given to me by my source. From time to time, I pull out my journal and peruse my entries. I have found that my mental complex remembers the mood and emotion of that recorded moment, and each time I reread my notes, it is as if the empowerment of that moment saturates my being afresh. A record of your vision can serve as future empowerment and a motivational vehicle that can be revisited when you're feeling dubious and emotionally drained during your pursuit of vision.

> *Write the vision, and make it plain on tablets,*
> *That he may run that read it.*
> (Habakkuk 2:2*a*)

Others will be motivated by reading your vision, and you, too, will be reignited and motivated to keep moving forward. Write it down and make it plain!

Factor 3: Venture

If everything we've discussed in this chapter is in place, then the venture is eminent. Where there is clarity of vision, there is immediate acceleration toward the known goal. When you have vision, it imparts adventure, and adventure involves venturing out, a daring undertaking, and the progression toward a known goal. Success cannot be achieved unless movement is initiated toward a preconceived destination or goal. In essence, the sooner you begin to work your vision plan, the sooner you will begin unfolding the unknown and the not-yet experienced victories that accompany vision ventures in life. Ventured victories are the progressive movement toward predetermined worthwhile goals. Ventures are stabilized by balanced, spiritual, and moral beliefs that provide the ability to enjoy the results of the vision quest.

When we finally get into motion, or act on our dreams, we gain confidence. Remember, inaction in all forms feeds fear. The longer you postpone movement toward your goals, the more resistance you build up ... devaluing the worth of your plans and goals. Once your plans and goals lose value mentally, you begin the slow process of aborting your purpose and destiny in life. Ability, vision, goals, and plans without action mean death to the reason for living. If there is no reason for living, there exists the haunting sense of worthlessness. Even in matters of faith, it has been said that, "Faith without works (venture) is dead" (James 2:20). Every great achievement in life is the result of an idea acted upon.

David J. Schwartz once said, "As you study people, both the successful and the, *just average*, you find they fall into two classes. The successful are active; we'll call them 'activationists.' The *just average*, the mediocre, and the unsuccessful are passive. We'll call them 'passivationists.' We can discover a success principle by studying both groups. Mr. Activationist is a doer. He takes action, gets things done, and follows through on ideas and plans. Mr. Passivationist is a 'don'ter.' He postpones doing things until he proves he shouldn't or, can't do them, or until it's too late."[29]

Venture in and of itself is action, and action must precede action. That is the law of nature. Nothing starts itself. Purpose begets destiny, destiny begets vision, vision begets motivation, and motivation begets the stimuli needed to jump-start or initiate. So from this equation, we set in motion the regenerating momentum of action begetting action.

It is time to do something about your plans. It is time to get into action! Your season of springtime possibilities mandates that you begin today actively pursuing your purpose, working your plans, and watching your vision unfold.

T. S. Eliot, a poet, critic, and dramatist wrote,

"Each venture is a new beginning,
A raid on the inarticulate with shabby equipment
Always deteriorating in the mess of imprecision of feeling."

Today is your day of new beginnings. As T. S. Elliot expressed, there will be a time that your venture will disturb those who have refused to venture—those who have chosen not to articulate their own dreams. Unfortunately, these dreams die or fade away in the battle of the mind and in the field of mixed emotions.

Factor 4: Avoid Excusitis, the Enemy of Vision

Nothing is as debilitating to the fulfillment of vision as excuses. Excuse is a deterrent to the development and success of any plan. It is a lethal disease. I personally embrace the diagnosis of this disease termed *Excusitis*. Every failed venture has it in its advanced form. Most individuals have at least a mild case of it. As stated in chapter 6, from personal experience and observation I made of other people's lives, excuses are characterized by:

- instinctive fleshly response to pressures with its primary purpose being, to gain relief from obligations or consequences,
- birthed out of comfort zone conditioning (you feel like you're going to lose something),

- negative responses magnifying your weaknesses rather than your strengths,
- cowardly ways to surrender to adversity,
- self-fulfilling prophesies ("Death and life is in the power of the tongue," Proverb 18:21),
- thieves who rob my tongue of faith affirmations and my mind of a confident   thought-life,
- the greatest enemies to success.

To avoid this disease you must deal with *past failures*, its primary source of life. If over a period of time there have been failed attempts to change or progress, you are likely to develop a mind-set that dictates that change and progress are not possible for you. Unfortunately, should this situation keep recurring, you will cease your attempts to change and take the roads that many have traveled in this life. Excuses may become a way of life; you develop a defeatist attitude and even see yourself as a constant failure. In time, your subconscious indiscriminately supports this negative self-image, recalling all the past failures you have experienced. This results in a paralysis of the will to change and acceptance of the status quo.

The visionary must place past failures in the past; that's where they belong. Today is a new day in your life. Old things have past away, and now is the springtime of your new self. Your future goals and plans require you to eliminate these past failures from your thought-life. They will rob you of development and paralyze your creative genius, all of which are vital to the visionary.

The visionary must learn to rise, conquer, and fulfill the plans and goals of life by lifting up his thoughts above all debilitating issues. Such debilitating issues tend to obstruct their special sight (vision) and their faith walk. When the visionary bathes his thoughts in truth, those thoughts are allied with God's power, and all difficulties are courageously met and prudently overcome. Thoughts bathed in purpose are seasonably planted, and they bloom, bringing forth fruit that does not fall prematurely to the ground, but rather, they await their season of spring, a time of beauty and divine perfection.

In the conclusion of this chapter on x-raying your vision, I must emphasize the importance of taking special precautions to protect your vision. It is common human nature to protect those things we cherish. You should by now have developed such a passion toward your purpose in life that you'll allow nothing to blur, taint, or take away your vision. Remain true to your vision, and never lose your desire, for to desire is to obtain, and to aspire is to achieve. So if the journey toward your vision seems tiring and unattainable, remember the remaining verses of Habakkuk 2:2–3 at the beginning of this chapter:

For the vision
Awaits an appointed time; it speaks of the end
And will not prove false. Though it linger,
Wait for it; it will certainly come
And will not delay.

16
Behold—A New Attitude: The Emotional Fruit of Necessary Changes

I will refine them like silver.

—Zechariah 13:9*b*

Came the Spring with all its splendor
All its birds and all its blossoms,
All its flowers, and leaves, and grasses.

—Longfellow

How beautiful it is to witness the rhythm of spring's effect on nature. This display symbolizes the fruit of refinement. Man, in all his wisdom and knowledge, could never produce such a phenomenal array of flowers, leaves, and grasses. All of creation harmonizes with this God-given splendor so aptly penned by Longfellow. Humanity worldwide is fascinated by this uniqueness, which appeals to all the senses. Your personal fruit of refinement exemplifies certain qualities and a beauty found only after successfully coming through the refining seasons. I can only compare it to the many scenes I am privileged to behold each day in south Florida.

It is like driving to the beach on an April spring day with an alluring breeze blowing through the car windows. It is crossing the intercoastal waterway, observing the ocean blow its breath upon the palm trees, arranging them into a bow as if they were escorting you to the beach, a place meticulously carved, irrigated, and measured with the Creator's unseen hand. It is a scene of flirting waves caressing the shore's symmetry … only to leave her wanton at the pull of undertow's jealous strength. It is the clouds in a quiet stroll across the sky's serene blue backdrop, reconciling yesterday's dark, thunderous moments of rain cry. It is the robin and the sparrow harmoniously performing their preflight serenade, complementing the ease found in this tranquil beauty. If nothing else, it is nature responding openly to her creator's refining touch.

You've made it through the four seasons of destiny's refining process in your life, and it is now time for you to exemplify the fruit of your refinement. There are so many wonderful qualities you've allowed to come into fruition through God's perfect processing of your life. These qualities exist to be embraced and enjoyed not only by the possessor but shared with, and embraced within, your sphere of influence. All beauty and truth that belong to the world remain hidden, except it proportionally finds expression through a vessel of creation. Like you, this vessel of creation must undergo the refining process in order to prepare for the flow of the divine, the rhythm of the Spirit of God moving through, around, and from the vessels to the world. The songwriter says, "Roll back the curtain of memories now and then," see where you were before refinement. There are individuals now in search of a model, someone who's been where they are but has shut out unwanted images and is an example of the "it can be done" mentality.

We've discussed many issues so far. Now we're at the point where the fruit of your renewed life must flow into all of your experiences. Your innate refinement has reached the point of *needed* release; the real you is eager to manifest. Lives have been orchestrated to intersect with you to experience what is possible in their lives. Your refinement has embraced the mind and Spirit of God, which freely flows within your being. The fruit of the Spirit of God that resides in you should now flow from you exemplifying your changed "personhood." So what are the fruit of refinement? They are outlined in the book of Galatians:

But the fruit of the Spirit is love, joy, peace, patience, kindness, goodness, faithfulness, gentleness and self-control. Against such things there is no law. Those who belong to Christ Jesus have crucified the sinful nature (died to old nature) with its passions desires. Since we live by the Spirit, let us keep in step (in rhythm) with the Spirit.

—Galatians 5:22–25

The burning question posed by most persons who have been through the pivotal challenges encountered during these seasons of life is, how do I know I've changed? The answer is found in the Scripture, "The tree is known by its fruit" (Matthew 12:33). It is amazing that there is such lack of understanding concerning the nine fruits of the Spirit. No wonder it is said that the simple things in life slay us. The simple things, if misunderstood, are the death of our progress. Without the fruit of the Spirit, nothing we do in life will bring us total fulfillment. There is no better way to bring closure to our seasons of fine-tuning and development than with discussing the importance of the fruit that will mark authentic change in our personhood and exemplify the infallible Holy Spirit's control of our lives.

The fruit of the Spirit is not as simple and common as the appearance. These are the authentic "etiquettes of renewal." They don't come easy; they are the results of the refining process. To understand this concept from this point on, I invite you to rethink your view of how you've defined them. Also, think about how you've expressed them in the past. You are different now, and everything about you should reflect a broader dimension. Remember, you're now viewing your "whole" life through the corrective lens of truth, not personal opinion or family and societal dictates.

Love

This fruit was discussed to some degree in chapter 14 in reference to your inner beauty. It is however, the foundation of all the others, so I will expand on it for what it's worth. Love is nondiscriminating; it defies all logic and resides in a realm beyond natural understanding. This foundational quality of inner beauty invites all to experience its warm acceptance and comforting embrace. A truly renewed and changed individual will move beyond the prognostic and rhetorical expression of love and begin to provide displayed works of love through unconditional acceptance, genuine forgiveness, encouragement, and heartfelt benevolence (see chapter 14).

God is the only one who reflects love in its pure state of perfection. But we can allow the perfecting process to expose us to the possibility of love's intended influence. You see, natural love is based on reciprocal love. Love, by extension for your consideration, is the degree to which you must demonstrate it to family, friends, neighbors, strangers, and even enemies. The transcending elements of this kind of love are found in a letter written to the church in Corinth:

Love is patient, love is kind. It does not envy, it does not boast, it is not proud. It is not rude, it is not self-seeking, it is not easily angered, it keeps no record of wrongs. Love does not delight in evil but rejoices with the truth. It always protects, always trust, always hopes, always perseveres. Love never fails.

When love is expressed as outlined in the above letter, it is obvious that a change has taken place in your life, and it is also difficult for anyone to deny this fact. Walter Trobisch, in his book *Love Is a Feeling to Be Learned*, concurs with my assessment that love that transcends is not natural, but is developed through the process of time: "Love is a feeling to be learned. It is deep longing and fulfillment. It is gladness and it is also pain: not one or the other. Happiness is only a part of love; a concept that has to be learned. Suffering belongs to love also. This is the mystery of love, its beauty and its burden. Love is a feeling to be learned."

Joy

The fruit joy is one of the most misunderstood and misinterpreted. Contrary to popular belief, joy is not something we experience, nor is it something that happens to us. Transcendent joy is like love: it is a choice. It is a decision we make about how we will respond to life's circumstances. Guillaume Apollinaire, a French poet, said, "Joy always comes after pain," which is in accordance with the scripture, "Weeping may remain for a night, but rejoicing comes in the morning" (Psalm 30:5 NIV). Joy seems to be a fruit whose essence is made known in the presence of mourning, pain, and despair.

Through an innate strength that is beyond our natural ability, we ascend into the eye of the storm. Though the winds of trouble and the tunnel of life's turbulence roar with a voice of hopeless destruction, the refined individual discovers and ascends into the calm … the eye of life's storm. It is here that we find "the unspeakable joy." It does not reason or make sense; it just is. It is the fruit that disregards what it sees, to embrace what it knows in the depth of spiritual truth. It knows that no matter what you face in life, "All things (good or bad) work together for our ultimate good."

Peace

Peace is the fruit that manifests itself in the form of a great calmness and equanimity of spirit when faced with turmoil or tragedy. It is a peace that passes all understanding. Like joy, peace transcends reason. I guess you can place the hand of peace in the hand of joy, because they walk side by side amid troubled times. Peace seems to reflect a state of being or composure, while joy evokes an emotional, and sometimes acted-out, response such as rejoicing. Peace is developed and nurtured as we grasp the sovereignty of God. In gasping the sovereignty of our divine source, we understand that our lives are orchestrated and protected by divine decree. So when we're instructed by Him, whose word never fails to, "Take no thought for tomorrow, for tomorrow will take thought for itself," we enjoy the peace that comes as a result of listening to the refiner's words, embracing them, believing them, clinging to them, clinging to Him, and living in His truth.

I am of the belief that men do not have peace in the world, or in their hearts, because they do not have peace with God. Nothing is settled until it is settled right, and nothing is settled right until it is settled with God. When I read the newspaper or view television, I'm exposed to the hate crimes, wars, and relational violations that plague our society. It is at this point Havner's statement rings out loud and clear. As much as the secular mind does not want to embrace God, it cannot deny the fact that there is a problem that exists in our world that only the God of peace can resolve.

Nothing reveals God's concern for peace more vividly than His decision to send His beloved Son to "guide our feet into the path of peace" (Luke 1:79; cf. Isaiah 2:4). Long before He was born, God's Son was given the title "Prince of Peace" (Isaiah 9:6). Through Jesus, the Christ, we are given three dimensions of peace: peace with God, peace with one another, and peace within ourselves. It is impossible to know genuine internal peace unless you also pursue peace with God and others.

Patience

"Bear with each other and forgive whatever grievances you may have against one another. Forgive as the Lord forgave you" (Colossians 3:13). It is imperative that we understand that patience and forgiveness are essentially proportionate one to another. Donna Partow, in *Becoming a Vessel God Can Use*, says that if you are an impatient person, "Examine your heart and you will discover that your real problem may be an unforgiving heart. Clinging to old hurts will not benefit you in any way. It will, however, prevent you from becoming the useful, overflowing vessel God designed you to be. Proverbs 19:11 says, 'A man's wisdom gives him patience; it is to his glory to overlook an offense.' When we are patient with others, we can forgive, we can overlook offenses. And when we forgive, we'll find we have an entire storehouse filled with patience."[30]

This fruit—patience—is a double-edged sword, for it relates not only to relationships but also to the acquisition of knowledge, the pursuit of goals and aspirations, and the period between solicited requests and their redeeming responses. Patience is a fruit that is developed. It is not natural to be patient. To some individuals, patience implies passivity, and they do not wish to be passive. Consider the times when you were in dire straits with no view of rescue, the times when you prayed for a need in your life to be met but the answer seemed not to be coming, or the time when you wanted to buy that house or automobile and the financing was not approved. Someone who has come through the seasons of life successfully says, "Oh be patient. It will come." Your initial response is not one of being overjoyed; instead, you're on the borderline of belief and disbelief. The counsel that was meant for encouragement sounds like discouragement to you.

To the unrefined individual, who has no interest in sharpening their personhood for destiny's use, a counsel of patience is an irritant and rarely a stimulus. In contrast, for the refined person of destiny, it is understood that patience is a fruit that gives us the wherewithal to rely on the innate spiritual power to assist us in the circumstances that are beyond our control. It is an understanding that the momentary pause in our life is that time when God, and God alone, is bringing into fruition what He expects for us and from us. It is that pause in our lives when God reveals His desires for us, and He assists in their manifestation. Patience is the key to the ability to reason. It is the key that turns our natural impatience from inappropriate response and action, in the place of helplessness and hopelessness, to a response of hope-filled appropriate action. Patience is an extension of faith that heightens our level of anticipation toward that which has been predetermined and prepared for us.

Kindness

Kindness is the greatest, yet the most fragile, of the spiritual fruit of refinement. The exploration of kindness and love is a journey on which one is sure to encounter deep spirituality before long. Here is why kindness is so fragile: it has the astonishing potential to grow into a most illuminating power, yet it often dies from neglect before it has a chance to sprout. This fruit is neglected because of its ability and power to make one vulnerable to a deeper spirituality. Kindness poses an annoying complication in the lives of people who are not interested or willing to have a deeper spiritual experience or relationship with the divine One. The refined individual always embraces the fruit of kindness, for it achieves deeper spirituality, the very goal of the seeker of meaning and purpose in life.

Jesus uses the parable of the good Samaritan as an illustration of the kindness principle. The Samaritan was an outcast. He or she was one of the wounded of society, yet was more likely to show kindness and hospitality than the privileged, which is what compassion means (Luke 10:1–37). Jesus, in telling this story to the lawyer described the Samaritan, as "the one who showed mercy," and we are commissioned to "go and do likewise." This use of the word *mercy* in this context causes curiosity, for the word *mercy* here suggests an unmerited kindness, something undeserved. This is simply not a natural kindness; it is a kindness in the face of an opportunity to do otherwise. The individual who has been refined will experience many opportunities to do otherwise but will be innately empowered to show mercy (kindness) where it is not deserved.

Goodness

Goodness is simply the innate essence to serve the moral excellence and desired behavior—upright end. I must reiterate that this kind of fruit is not natural either; it takes hard work. The Bible tells us that we are to, "Make every effort ... to add to our faith goodness ... and brotherly kindness." "Make every effort" implies that this is hard work. We cannot passively wait to be filled with kindness and goodness. We are to actively seek to be filled. If we possess these qualities in increasing measure, they will keep us from being ineffective and unproductive in our knowledge of the divine.

Faithfulness

Faith is the focal point of all that we aspire to in life. Success without faith is meaningless and often personally debilitating. According to *Strong's Exhaustive Concordance*, a faithful person is stable, trustworthy, established, certain, and true. To be faithful means you know exactly what you believe, and you stand by it. The fruit, faithfulness, heralds from persons of purpose, a sense of divine "knowing." They sense that they have been put on earth with particular gifts and goals and are confident that whatever destiny has purposed for them, that is where they are headed. Faith, being an innate quality of God, is a source of transcending thoughts that can reshape our attitudes and behaviors.

King Solomon addressed the issue of faithfulness as a treasure to cleave to: "Let Love and faithfulness never leave you; bind them around your neck, write them on the tablet of your heart. Then you will win favor and a good name in the sight of God and man" (Proverbs 3:3–4).

Gentleness

Nothing magnifies this particular fruit like the following passage: "Your beauty should not come from outward adornment, such as braided hair and the wearing of gold/jewelry and fine clothes. Instead, it should be that of your inner self, the unfading beauty of a gentle and quiet spirit, which is of great worth in God's sight" (1 Peter 3:3–4). The fruit gentleness reflects a pleasant disposition, cordial and congenial. It can also be connected with that of kindness and goodness, expanding its dimension in relation to a tender composure that has the power to melt away hardheartedness. Gentleness approaches/confronts any and all situations and relationships with a humble heart. It is the outward expression of an inward reality: a heart that is humbled and a life that is emptied of self and yielded to the One who is divine and sovereign.

Self-Control

Self-control is the fruit of refinement that is exemplified by restraint, the ability to control your behavior, especially in terms of impulses and reactions. Emerging from the fires of refinement, you should be able to control yourself and not allow anger or any other negative emotion to immobilize your rational capacity. Outward attempts at self-control are futile. Once again, this is a fruit of spiritual renewal, an innate change. When you take a closer look at self-control, it really isn't "self"-control; it is your renewed spiritual nature assisting or empowering you to subdue and exercise dominion over any aspect of your human nature that tends to respond to life in an "out of control" manner.

Anger and negative emotions are not the only aspects of human nature that need to be brought under the dominion of the refining fruit, self-control. Any overindulgent behavior is a prime candidate for admittance to the "Clinic of Self-Control." I doubt that anyone would disagree with me when I say that there are learned, generational vices in our live that we all must watch out for. Vices are learned through family/generational cycles that reflect them as a response to life, or as coping agents. They are also learned through relationships from which we desire acceptance. These vices have the potential to dominate and control our personhood. Following are just a few them:

- fear
- no inner spiritual peace
- abnormal passions
- violent temper
- nervousness and apprehension
- instability
- chronic emotional turmoil
- addiction to alcohol, nicotine, sex, and drugs
- gluttony

These represent the "fruit" of the "root" of human nature with no spiritual refinement; it is *flesh (human nature) out of control.* The refined individual exemplifies self-control in all aspects of his life. This person utilizes the insight of spiritual wisdom to correctly identify uncontrolled centers of power and submit them to the innate quality or fruit that can only come from the seasons that are necessary for change.

In conclusion of this chapter, I must say how extraordinary

you are. Look at the wonderful jewels you've extracted from the process of refinement! Like a woman who has been given a perfectly cut diamond, be excited and honored about the new you shaped by the skillful hand of God. Show yourself to the world! Exemplify the refined features of your new life. Would you hide a magnificent jewel that you've discovered was right under your nose these many years? Likewise, don't allow the brilliance of what you've discovered to be hidden or fade away. You've been cut and polished. Now you are set in the display window of the world to be seen by all. Your life will expose the possibilities available to yielded souls in search of the who, why, and where of their lives, those in search of—truth.

Do not cover it, expose it.
Do not keep it to yourself, share it.

Epilogue

*A man's mind may be likened to a garden, which may be
intelligently cultivated or allowed to run wild …*

*As a gardener cultivates his plot, keeping it free from weeds,
and growing the flowers and fruits which he requires, so may a man
tend the garden of his mind, weeding out all the wrong, useless,
and impure thoughts, and cultivating toward perfection
the flowers and fruits of right, useful, and
pure thoughts.*

—James Allen

The Human Predicament
(Security and Significance)

But the man or woman who lives only for the love and attention of others is never satisfied, at least, not for long. Despite our efforts, we will never find lasting, fulfilling peace if we must continually prove ourselves to others. Our desire to be loved and accepted is a symptom of a deeper need, the need that frequently governs our behavior and is the primary source of our emotional pain. Often unrecognized, this is our need for self-worth.

—Robert S. McGee

I trust you have been challenged by our journey through the perfecting process of life's changing seasons. Most of what I wanted to tell you in this final section was concluded in the last chapter. You can get started now on building and strengthening your new life, or if you choose, you may join me in one last discussion. The last subject I will briefly deal with on the perfecting seasons has to do with anchoring your life. The anchor I speak of is resolving the issues of security and significance.

Necessary Changes was to be a model by which anyone at any point in their life could identify where they fit in the scheme of life. I wanted to share with you the seasons that were relevant to events happening in your own life that threaten your security and your significance. The book was also to help you focus on how your thought-life affects your emotional, relational, and spiritual development. The "human" or the "fallen nature" of mankind prompts our thought-life to seek guidance and understanding concerning life through the experiences and philosophies of each other. As we have seen, that can be a tragedy.

Because we are all fallible, it is safe to assume that the counsel we offer each other from a worldly opinion or perspective is usually the crowning cause of our errors and disappointments in life. Firstly, this is true due to the fact that human philosophies are usually prejudicial in orientation and relative to a specific time as well as a particular circumstance. Secondly, this is true because yesterday's antidotes may be obsolete, thus compounding today's problems. In the end, we find ourselves right back at the beginning of our dilemma. This dilemma is best described in the academic circles of psychology as the *human predicament*. According to the psychological and theological perspectives of the human predicament, mankind is in search of two major aspects of life: *significance* and *security*.

These two aspects of the human predicament are the motivating factors to many of our hurts and failures in life; it raises the questions of relevance and begins the search for the answers. Unfortunately, life without proper guidance most times expands our human predicament to unbearable degrees. For this reason, nature's instinct, otherwise called survival instinct, steps forward to provide protection for the existence and continuity of life. This is sometimes advocated as a noble, aggrandizement of personal fortitude and even a preferred way of life. But here is the reality of that illusion: unless proper counsel is received and appropriately applied, the survival instinct will ultimately develop into emotional crutches that create a generic sense of security and significance.

Robert S. McGee explains it this way: "We all develop elaborate defense mechanisms to block pain and gain significance. We suppress emotions and are compulsive perfectionists. We drive ourselves to succeed, or we withdraw and become passive. We attack people who hurt us, and we punish ourselves when we fail. We try to say clever things to be accepted. We help people so that we will be appreciated; and we say and do countless other things. A sense of need usually propels us to look for an alternative. We may have the courage to examine ourselves and may desperately want to change but may be unsure of how and where to start. We may refuse to look honestly within for fear of what we might find, or we may be afraid that even if we discover what's wrong, nothing can help us."[31] That is, nothing in our personal strength.

Myles Monroe, a noted author and president of the Bahamas Faith Ministries International in Nassau, Bahamas, said to me at a conference in Miami, Florida, "The key to understanding life is not in life itself, but in the Source of life." This truth has been the central thrust of this book. The heart of what I have written has been to enlighten you to the fact that the seasons of life are God's tool for assisting you in emptying yourselves of your self, preparing you for the adventures in your life. Once the emptying of self is achieved, the infinite One fills you with His Spirit, and all of the provisions that you will ever need to feel innately secure, have a sense of significance, and fulfill your destiny in life.

I sincerely hope that this book has served as a tool for giving you a fresh perspective as you move toward finding meaning in your life experiences. And, that you come to the realization that mankind needs something or someone larger and stronger than feelings to carry us through the tough times. As long as there is life, manifestation of these tough times is inevitable. Your walk with me through this manuscript has left me wondering what must be going through your mind as you're about to complete the journey through the last of these pages. Maybe you're asking yourself some questions similar to those I asked when I was experiencing and developing the concept of paralleling nature's seasons to life's pivotal periods. My chief question was, After I've gone through the four seasons of destiny's perfection, then what? This is an honest and most profound question. The answer is just as honest. I guess the best way to explain this would be to begin with one word that sums up the answer. It is the word "commencement," which is more popularly used in an educational venue. Commencement literally means to come into existence, to begin. In the educational setting, it is the simultaneous ending and beginning of a continuous process. Primarily, the spirit of the word is that there is no definitive conclusion.

So if you have asked the question what next, then the answer is that there is no definitive conclusion to your seasons in life. Just as nature's seasons are cyclical, changing and flowing from one to another, year after year, so are the seasons of your life. The principle concept here is that we all have issues that must be dealt with throughout our lifetime. All these issues can never be exposed and dealt with in one cycle; it is a lifetime endeavor. Each successive year you spend cleansing and working through these issues yields a higher level of personal accomplishment, maturity, and fulfillment of intermediate goals toward your ultimate purpose in life. The issues that you are confronted with at this very moment in your life are the priority issues for this seasonal cycle. The reason this is a lifetime journey is because we are constantly evolving. The longer we live, the more we discover about ourselves. So be patient with yourself and the process.

Having read this book, you should recognize that I am a committed Christian and firm believer of biblical principles, which I know is the source of excellence and success in my life. If you've never made a spiritual commitment, I am now extending this opportunity to you for your consideration. There is much in the press these days concerning the Christ. With Mel Gibson's movie *The Passion of the Christ*, I refuse to imagine that there is an individual in the United States of America who doesn't know about Jesus Christ and/or the purpose of His life on earth. With that thought, I bring closure to our journey. I share with the renowned author and motivator Norman Vincent Peale a sentiment from his book *The Positive Power of Imaging*. Permit me to sow this sentiment in your heart:

The most wonderful thing that can happen to any of us is to have that most profound of all experiences—to know Jesus Christ personally. You can hear about Him all your life and never really know Him. You can believe that He lived and respect Him and honor Him as a great historical figure and still only know Him academically. But when at last you find Him and experience His reality, then for you He comes out of the stained-glass windows and out of history and becomes your personal Savior, then you can walk through all manner of darkness and pain and trouble and be unafraid.

I hope this book has provided some stimulating and thought-provoking information that will promote what I call "the growth process." I wish you well on your journey and beyond. I am pleased and thankful that our paths have crossed, and I hope you feel the same way, too.

If this book has challenged or enlightened you in any way, why not share it with a family member, friend, or just someone you know?

Endnotes

Chapter 1

1. Microsoft® Encarta® Encyclopedia 2002. © 1993–2001 Microsoft Corporation.

2. Kay Arthur, *As Silver Refined*. (Colorado Springs, Colo.: Waterbrook Press, 1997), 28.

Chapter 2

3. Joel Goldsmith, *Practicing the Presence*. (New York: HarperCollins, 1958), 10.

Chapter 3

4. James Allen, *As a Man Thinketh* (New York: Grosset & Dunlap, 2006), 5.

Chapter 4

5. Microsoft® Encarta® Encyclopedia 2002. © 1993–2001 Microsoft Corporation.

Chapter 7

6. Allen, *As a Man Thinketh*, 5.

Chapter 8

7. William Hines, *Leaving Yesterday Behind.* (Fearn, Tain, Ross-shire, Scotland: Christian Focus Publication, 1997), 65.

8. Eric Fellman, *The Power Behind Positive Thinking.* (New York: HarperCollins, 1996), 181–82.

9. Robert S. McGee, *The Search for Significance.* (Nashville, Tenn.: Word Publishing, 1998), 23.

10. Patrick Morley, *The Man in the Mirror.* (Grand Rapids, Mich.: Zondervan Publishing, 1997), 37.

Chapter 9

11. Goldsmith, *Practicing the Presence*, 96.

Chapter 10

12. David J. Schwartz, *The Magic of Thinking Big* (New York: Simon & Schuster, 1987), 48.

13. I. V. Hilliard, *Mental Toughness for Success* (Houston: Light Publications, 1996), 108–109.

Chapter 11

14. Morley, *The Man in the Mirror*, 44.

15. Frank B. Minirth and Paul D. Meier, *Counseling and the Nature of Man* (Grand Rapids, Mich.: Baker, 1982), 13.

16. Frank Delitzsch, *A System of Biblical Psychology* (Grand Rapids, Mich.: Baker, 1966), 116–17.

17. Milliard J. Erickson, *Christian Theology* (Grand Rapids, Mich.: Baker, 1998), 539.

18. Kenneth E. Hagin, *Man on Three Dimensions* (Tulsa, Okla.: RHEMA, 1973), 7.

19. Kahlil Gibran, *The Prophet* (New York: Alfred A. Knopf, 1923), 54–55.

Chapter 12

20. Erickson, *Christian Theology*, 490.

21. Ibid., 492.

22. Myles Munroe, *In Pursuit of Purpose.* (Shippensburg, Pa.: Destiny Image, 1992), 5.

23. Ibid., 8.

24. Hilliard, *Mental Toughness for Success*, 105–108.

25. Charles Colson, *The Body: Being Light in the Darkness* (Dallas: Word Publishing, 1992), 185–86.

Chapter 13

26. Floyd H. Barackman, *Practical Christian Theology* (Grand Rapids, Mich.: Kregel, 1981), 69.

27. Schwartz, *The Magic of Thinking Big*, 108.

Chapter 14

28. Microsoft* Encarta* Encyclopedia 2002. © 1993–2001 Microsoft Corporation.

Chapter 15

29. Schwartz, *The Magic of Thinking Big*, 135.

Chapter 16

30. Donna Partow, *Becoming a Vessel God Can Use* (Minneapolis: Bethany House, 1996), 153.

Epilogue

31. McGee, *The Search for Significance*, 3.

Bibliography

Allen, James. *As a Man Thinketh*. New York: Grosset & Dunlap, 2006.

Arthur, Kay. *As Silver Refined*. Colorado Springs, Colo.: Waterbrook Press, 1997.

Barackman, Floyd H. *Practical Christian Theology*. Grand Rapids, Mich.: Kregel, 1981.

Colson, Charles. *The Body: Being Light in the Darkness*. Dallas: Word Publishing, 1992.

Delitzsch, Frank. *A System of Biblical Psychology*. Grand Rapids, Mich.: Baker, 1966.

Erickson, Millard J. *Christian Theology*. Grand Rapids, Mich.: Baker, 1998.

Fellman, Eric. *The Power Behind Positive Thinking*. New York: HarperCollins, 1996.

Gibran, Kahlil. *The Prophet*. New York: Alfred A. Knopf, 1923.

Goldsmith, Joel. *Practicing the Presence*. New York: HarperCollins, 1958.

Hagin, Kenneth E. *Man on Three Dimensions*. Tulsa, Okla.: RHEMA, 1973.

Hilliard, I. V. *Mental Toughness for Success*. Houston: Light Publications, 1996.

Hines, William. *Leaving Yesterday Behind*. Fearn, Tain, Ross-shire, Scotland: Christian Focus Publisher, 1997.

Jeeves, Malcolm A. *Human Nature at the Millennium*. Grand Rapids, Mich.: Baker Books, 1997.

McGee, Robert S. *The Search for Significance*. Nashville, Tenn.: Word Publishing, 1998.

Microsoft Encarta Encyclopedia 2002. 1993–2001 Microsoft Corporation.

Minirth, Frank B., and Paul D. Meier. *Counseling and the Nature of Man*. Grand Rapids, Mich.: Baker, 1982.

Morley, Patrick. *The Man in the Mirror*. Grand Rapids, Mich.: Zondervan, 1997.

Munroe, Myles. *In Pursuit of Purpose*. Shippensburg, Pa.: Destiny Image, 1992.

Partow, Donna. *Becoming a Vessel God Can Use*. Minneapolis: Bethany House, 1996.

Schwartz, David J. *The Magic of Thinking Big*. New York: Simon & Schuster, 1987.